Listener in the Snow

The Practice and Teaching of Poetry

Mark Statman

Teachers & Writers Collaborative

New York

Library of Congress Cataloging-in-Publication Data

Statman, Mark, 1958–
    Listener in the snow : the practice and teaching of poetry / Mark Statman
        p. cm
    Includes bibliographical references.
    ISBN 0-915924-59-5 (alk. paper)
    1. Poetry--Study and teaching. 2. Poetry--Authorship. 3. Poetry--Explication.

PN1101 .S68 2000
808.1'07--dc21   99-054406

Teachers & Writers Collaborative
5 Union Square West
New York, NY 10003-3306

Cover and page design: Christopher Edgar

Cover art: detail from *What Scatterina Gave Me* by Katherine Koch

Author's photo: Joe Schuyler

Printed by Philmark Lithographics, New York, N.Y.

Table of Contents

Permissions

Acknowledgments

Thanks to:

My editors, Ron Padgett and Chris Edgar, for support, direction, and attentiveness;

Kenneth Koch, whose questions, commentary, and challenges helped clarify my thinking; and to Karen Koch as well, who provided an educator's insight;

Mary Crowley, for a close, enthusiastic reading of an earlier version of my manuscript;

People at Teachers & Writers, present and past, including Nancy Shapiro, Lynn Michau, Jill Jackson, Elizabeth Fox, Simon Kilmurry, and Pat Padgett, and fellow writers, Larry Fagin, Julie Patton, Kurt Lamkin, and Christian McEwen;

Colleagues at Eugene Lang College, in particular my officemate of more than ten years, Greg Tewksbury, for our talks on poetry, pedagogy, and politics;

All the principals I've worked with, particularly Mike Wolk (Park Avenue School), Senta Stich (Daniel Webster Magnet School), and the late Robert W. Wells (P.S. 49, Bronx) for their leadership, friendship, and continuous commitment to poetry in the classroom;

All the teachers I've worked with throughout the years, for the privilege of being in their classrooms, and, in particular, Mark Ceconi, artist, poet, and science teacher extraordinaire, for the teaching talk on our mountain-bike rides;

The students, in all the schools, for their poems, here and elsewhere;

Luisa Giugliano and Jane Hohenberger LeCroy, former students, now friends, whose poetry and commitment to teaching and children have reinvigorated my own;

Katie Porter, for Great Spruce Head Island, and Suds and Mary Ann Elwood, for Nimrod;

Stuart Statman, who, when the computer said it could not, made sure it did anyhow;

Katherine Koch, for love and critiques of endless revisions, and whose grumpy advice brought my head out of the clouds.

For Katherine and Jesse

Preface

by Kenneth Koch

This likeable, straightforward, and surprising book brings together the practice of poetry and the teaching of poetry. One gets to know Mark Statman as a person and as a writer and also as the teacher that these two have enabled him to become. That is one of the great and original clarifications this book offers. What one can teach children about writing poetry is of course what one knows oneself about it, and what one knows about it comes from who one is and from how one writes and what one has written. Teachers' day-to-day lives as well as their philosophic concerns are bound to affect their conception of what poetry is, what good poetry is, what is worth teaching about it to children, and how best to go about doing that. In other books I know on the subject, those connections may be implicit but they are hidden. Here, in Mark Statman's book, one gets to find out where the poetry lessons are coming from. This kind of revelation is refreshing, and it's also brave. Conceptions of poetry (and even of teaching) are most often presented as absolutes; in showing where his ideas come from, along with giving samples of his own poems and stories, Statman is stepping out from behind the screen of Poetry Wisdom and showing himself as just what he is: a particular individual with his own particular and sometimes idiosyncratic ideas about poetry and about life.

Every poet-teacher is in fact such an individual; so that if the reader thinks "Oh well, that's just you, and so what good is it to me?" the answer is that the connection between this teacher (Statman) and the others is that all are engaged in integrating their lives and their poetry and their teaching, and that this book shows one person successfully doing it. So one can find out how to do it for oneself—not by copying assignments, for example, but by seeing here a way to create assignments of one's own.

If the integration of person, poet, and teacher is one of the striking revelations of *Listener in the Snow*, another—just as important and clearly related to this first one—is the integration of the poems the children write and their understanding of and participation in the ideas and the feelings in the poems. Many books about this kind of teaching tend to concentrate on having the children do exercises, of which the main effects, if they are successful, will be the children's delight in saying things they haven't said before and in discovering that they are able to say them. There are likely to be, as well, such accidental felicities as may result from their using a language that, one might say, "knows more" than they do. Their partial knowledge of the meanings and associations of words may result in fresh and suggestive ways of using them. The children can then be shown what they've done and enabled to appreciate its value. These are very good things; and, in his lessons, Mark Statman does them all. But what he adds to this teaching is a more complete integration of what the children know and feel with what they write. Subjects—like time, silence, traveling, loss—that are talked about in the poems that are the center of the lessons, are also talked about in class both before the children write and after. In this way, not only are the young writers stirred by memories and fresh ideas, but they will then come to the writing of their poems with some knowledge, even some mastery, of the subject, which enables them to write with the confidence born of experience and of independent reflection. Just as class discussions connect what the children write to what they know from experience, another part of the teaching connects what they write to the other things they are doing in school. If they are studying African geography, for example, the teacher will find a way to enter this subject imaginatively by means of poetry, or to take off from it and go somewhere else. To help make such connections most effective, Statman spends time talking to the classroom teachers, finding out what the children are doing, what interests them, where their interest may need to be strengthened.

As a result, the work of the regular teacher and that of the poet are brought together. Mark Statman comes into a school not as a refreshing novelty or an aesthetic entertainer, though he is these to some extent, but also as a new and important part of the curriculum (whether those who planned the curriculum are aware of it at first or not).

One can hardly not be elated at the prospect of this kind of teaching, which adds poetry to the children's lives—and adds it in a way that deepens what they are learning, in and out of school.

To discover how to do all this requires, of course, a knowledgeable and dedicated teacher. The chapter on revision alone shows how much Mark Statman knows of the techniques of poetry as well as of the ideas and feelings that go into it, and how well he knows how to talk about these things to his students—and to his readers. One could go through this book and learn just from his teaching strategies to be a better and wiser teacher. However, thanks to its clarity, its openness, and its warmth, this book shows us more than that. It shows how what happens in a classroom can become more fully a part of a child's true education, and how poetry can contribute to that effect. Since, as Ernest Hemingway remarks in *Death in the Afternoon*, there is no going backward in pleasure, teaching poetry may never be the same again.

Introduction

I. The Practice of Poetry

The Surprising Flowers

Summer of pretty colors
come to my backyard

Bloom the colors
of the sun

And the tasty plum
yellow, orange, purple

Bring me great happiness
surprising flowers

—Christine Schwall, fourth grade

I've been teaching writing in the schools—elementary, junior high, high school and college, urban, suburban, rural—since 1983. This book is about that work. But it's not simply a "how-to" book. It's not that I'm against how-to's. I've used a lot of them and have contributed lessons to some. But the focus for these books is often extremely limited. The writer introduces a lesson, discusses how the writer has taught it (and how another teacher might then also teach it), and shows some of the poems the students have written as a result.

My approach has been to look much more closely at *why* this writing happens, to connect the practical (here are things that you can do in a classroom) and the more aesthetic or pedagogical or personal (here's why you do them). My method isn't to give students tips on how to write nor is it to trick them into doing so. Instead, it's to get them to understand the *practice* of poetry: what it means to make it, how one does it, and why. I want them to see why *they* might want to write, why it might be interesting, pleasurable, challenging, provocative. I want to help them find how they'd like to do their own writing, to get them thinking about the things other poets and writers have thought about. I ask them to think and talk about themselves, their lives, their reality, their imaginations.

1

We also talk about ideas, the nature of things in the world and out of the world. What the students say in these discussions becomes the starting point for their poetry writing.

The success I've had with this approach is thus more than just about the particular lessons I've developed. It's about the personal and very collaborative process that led to those lessons. To write about a lesson without placing it in the context from which it was developed leaves out the why of the process: why this poem, these ideas, at this specific moment, with these specific students?

This why is a major question in *Listener in the Snow*. I wonder not simply about the materials and the ideas I teach, but why I teach them. I think about why, when I'm reading a book of poems, one of them jumps out at me and causes me to think: That is the one I want the kids to read. In the book, I explore why I thought some subject was important or necessary to talk about in the classroom. My main goal in my teaching has been to help create a culture of writing in the classroom and school, and to see how, in doing so, we could use that culture to write and talk about the ideas, emotions, meanings, and issues in our lives. As a result, the work in *Listener in the Snow* reflects not only on my teaching practices, but on my motivations for them, raising the question not only of how I teach the material I'm interested in but why I'm interested in it and why I think that interest makes it important to others.

The result has been that I've expanded the usual time frame for the development of a lesson. I start by talking about where the idea for the writing idea came from, how that first idea might have appeared in my own thinking and writing, how I thought about it in terms of the teaching that might happen (the development of the writing idea), what actually happened in the classrooms, and what the students finally wrote. As a follow-up I think about what the writing the students did might have meant to them. By providing insight into the why of what I teach about writing, and using that to demonstrate lessons (and their results), I hope to give other writers, teachers, and students a fresh sense of what they can do in their own writing and teaching.

Writing about all this has been an unusual experience. It has meant thinking a lot about myself, about what interests me in writing, in reading, and in living, and in ways that I hadn't previously connected to my teaching. It has given me the chance, too, to examine the interconnectednesses that I have always known to exist in all these different areas but whose existence I'd never taken the time to wonder about. These examinations have taught me a lot about myself; I've remembered things I hadn't expected to, thought about ideas and people in ways unanticipated. Writing these essays has been a kind of beginning for me in understanding my work as a writer and teacher much more clearly, much more completely.

I've noticed in my teaching, as well as in my own writing, there are occasional sudden veerings: I plan to do one thing and, suddenly, because of the weather, the hour of the day, the students, sometimes even because of the writing plan itself, something else happens. As Frank O'Hara noted about writing poetry, you have to go on your nerve, you have to let the writing that is going to happen happen, even if it isn't quite what you expected. Because the essays are about the why of my teaching, they're also about me and my own poetry and fiction. What I teach about writing is what I practice as a writer. Though I don't often use my own writing as models for the students, I always do the assignments I ask them to do, sometimes before the lesson, in anticipation, sometimes after it, because of inspiration. Sometimes a lesson will come out of a piece I'm working on; I'm exploring an idea and I want to see how the students handle it.

The essays also include the work of the writers I've used as models for my teaching and the poetry and fiction the students have written in response; that is, each chapter has its how-to section. But my interest is not in introducing a lesson that someone else might replicate exactly. Instead, it's in introducing an idea or series of ideas that might inspire other writers, teachers, and students in their thinking about what they might want to bring to their work.* In addition to offering specific writing lessons for the classroom, I hope these essays influence others to think about their own teaching and writing, how they happen, and why, and, in doing this kind of reflecting, how to become better at both.

---

* I notice, for example, that Latin American and Latino poets play a large role in my teaching. This is not because of an aestheic agenda I have: it just happens that I've spent a good deal of time in the last ten years or so travelling and working in Mexico and Central and South America, and I've been very interested in the poets of these places.

II. Teaching Poetry Writing: Getting Collaborative

Firecrackers

As I listen to the
firecrackers and my dad
holds me tight and
my dad holds me tight
and I say I feel
safe in your arms

    —Katie Schember, third grade

Most of the teaching I refer to comes out of work I've done since 1985 as a teaching artist for Teachers & Writers Collaborative and as poet/writer-in-residence at the Daniel Webster Magnet School in New Rochelle, New York. My work for Teachers & Writers, ranging from 50 to 120 days each school year, has been in some wonderful, diverse, and difficult places, schools in Brooklyn, Manhattan, the Bronx, and Queens, Long Island, New Jersey, and Connecticut. Most of the teaching has involved reading and writing poetry. I've also taught fiction writing, playwriting, journalism, and creative and critical prose in more than thirty schools, working with hundreds of teachers and thousands of students from pre-K to high school.

Of the schools I've mentioned, there are three I'd like to single out because of how successful the work has been there: the above-mentioned Webster School, the Park Avenue School in North Bellmore on Long Island, and P.S. 49 in the South Bronx. Unlike most schools, which view the artist-in-residence program as one that is valuable but also an add-on, these three elementary schools, through careful collaborative planning, have seen the work of the poet-in-residence as an integral part of their curricula; in each school for at least eight years, I've taught for a minimum of twenty-five days. What this has meant over the course of these years is that I've been able to work with almost every grade level, with almost every teacher and student and not just for one or two years, but for three, four, or five. It's meant watching and helping young people grow up, working with one student and then a younger sister or brother (and then another, another). It's meant meeting parents, becoming a part of the school community, attending parties and graduations, even a wedding!

What develops through all this consistency and commitment to writing is the emergence of a genuine culture of writing, in which students, faculty, and administration all see creative writing as a fundamental component of *everyone's* educational life. The young writers enjoy writing creatively and critically. Over these years, they've gotten better at it, more comfortable with what they can do, and more willing to be challenged. They've also given me a chance to experiment with different poems and different approaches and, in knowing that they were part of an experiment, they have assisted me in thinking critically about what was happening.

These young writers have grown to appreciate writing in ways that are subtle, sophisticated, and happy. They see reading and writing imaginatively as normal, and they can come to both activities without the fear generated by ignorance (*What is this?*) and with the confidence generated by familiarity (*Look at what this is!*). They know that writing can be difficult, that it often ought to be, but they also know, at least by the time they leave elementary school, that they can do it because they have been doing it *for years*.

The majority of the students and classrooms I refer to in the book are on the elementary school level, the level at which I've had the chance to teach these ideas and themes with depth and consistency. However, experience has shown me that almost all of what I write about here can be explored at any level (for example, recently my freshman college students wrote some wonderful poems about silence and reality, and a class consisting mainly of college sophomores and juniors surprised me with the intensity of their poems about hoping). In this book, I have tried to talk about what I might do differently with students of different ages when it seemed that the difference in age would change how I presented the lesson.

My teaching approach is pretty much the same on all levels. It is process- and labor-intensive and highly collaborative. What I do in a classroom depends heavily on what the students, teachers, and administrators with whom I work have decided that they want or need and what I in turn can do to help fulfill those wants and needs. Almost all of the writing ideas, writing lessons, and student work in this book are a result of those collaborations.

Often, what everyone desires is easy and obvious. During planning meetings with teachers and administrators, we talk about the writing the students have been doing and will be doing during the school year.* Teachers talk about their strengths and weaknesses as teachers of writing, and I do the same. We talk about the subjects the students are studying that year. Many schools have begun to develop grade-level themes that become the center for the year's curriculum: justice, peace, communication, conflict resolution, and so on. I try to learn as much as I can about how and when those themes are explored. Finding out about all these things allows me to figure out the ways in which I can add another perspective to the curriculum. If one grade is focusing on the environment, I might bring in Gabriela Mistral's "The Helpers" (see chapter 9) with its strange take on identity and its identification with nature. If a class is studying the rain forest, Elizabeth Bishop's "Questions of Travel" (in chapter 6) is a fine descriptive poem with echoes of the Brazilian rain forest, which asks the reader to wonder, along with the poet, at how we look at places foreign to ourselves. If studies include the ocean, I'll bring in Pablo Neruda's "The Sea" (in chapter 6), which challenges the students when it says, "[the sea] doesn't seem like much to young people. . . ."

There are other ways I try to fit into the life of the school and classroom. Sometimes I talk about the difference between scientific and poetic theory.† For classes working on historical figures, we write dramatic, creative point-of-view poems (chapter 9), allowing the students to apply what they know from one area of the curriculum to another in an unusual way. I won't teach a poem, though, just because I think it would be "useful," that it would make a good "lesson." I teach poems I like: for what

---

* Often a school will express the hope that having a poet-in-residence will raise reading and writing scores; although I doubt the ability of these tests to assess authentic reading and writing skills—the tests seem to focus more on a student's ability to follow instructions than on any kind of creative and critical reading and writing—I do know that having a poet in the classroom can help in the development of students' ability to think and write.

† Although I don't include poetic versus scientific theory in *Listener in the Snow*, the reader can find my essay "Poetic Theory and the End of Science," along with other useful exercises, in *Old Faithful: 18 Writers Present Their Favorite Writing Assignments* (New York: Teachers & Writers Collaborative, 1995).

they have to say and how they say it.* I'm not just interested in giving the students models for inspiring their ideas, I also want the models to inspire how they write. Furthermore, I want the poems to make sense to the kids in terms of their own lives.

Using the school curriculum as a starting point for my work invites the classroom teacher's collaboration more completely because it includes his or her own work in the teaching I'm going to do. By taking what I know about writing and literature and putting it in the context of the classroom, I demonstrate that imaginative writing can be as usual, as normal, as regular, as anything else students do in the course of the school-day. Including their "usual" knowledge helps the students understand the "unusual" material I might bring in. They can read and write with great depth because what I'm presenting may be new in many ways, but it is not completely unfamiliar. This allows teachers to do follow-up when I'm not there because they can see how what we've done together relates to their regular work. It also helps teachers to see that they can do creative writing across their curriculum; by watching me do it, they're able to figure out how it can be done in other places and in other ways.

My lessons are developed not only with the teachers, but with the students as well. I want them to like the work we do together and I want them to feel challenged by it. I also want them to challenge me, to tell me what they want, need, and think of what we're doing. In one junior high school classroom in Washington Heights in upper Manhattan, the students objected that for too many weeks in a row the poems and themes, while relevant to the work of the class, were also too harsh and depressing. They wanted to know, couldn't we read and talk about something good, beautiful, or happy? Another time, in a classroom in the Bronx, while discussing simile and metaphor, one student, reflecting on the comparison "old as the hills," asked me why adults always talked about the "good old days." Other students wondered the same thing. So I asked them what they thought the reasons were. A great discussion folllowed about the past, memory, and the future, as did some wonderful

---

* This attention to form and language is obviously best done with poems written in English; since I'm the translator of the Spanish poems included in *Listener in the Snow*, I'm able to talk about form a little more carefully in some of those examples, but for most of the poems translated into English, the themes and images of the poem sometimes take precedence over the formal considerations.

new poems, rich with simile and metaphor, all revolving around this unexpected topic.

III. Inspiration: The Use of Models

The Writer I Am

I am the writer
I am the writer that has the
power in my words, in my poems
I am the time you waste
I am the poet that makes you sweat.
I am the writer of the sound all around
I have the power to create
I have the power to destroy
I am not the mathematic you want
I am not the scientist you have
I am not the summer or the spring
I am the poet
I am the spirit that haunts you in the night
I am the death I am
the life I
am your poet.

—*Julia Ayres, fifth grade*

My usual method of developing a specific teaching lesson is to consider the themes a class is studying and to see if I know any poem or story that might provide a relevant and interesting model for the students. I believe strongly in using models. Rather than trying to define for students what poetry is, I show it to them, to let them see the various possibilities for poetry. I don't think using models limits students. When I was an undergraduate at Columbia University in the late 1970s, Kenneth Koch, who asked his students there to write poetry that was influenced by or responded to the work of poets he assigned, noted that you could never be influenced by someone too much. Meaning, I think, that if someone's poetry or someone's ideas helped you to become a better writer, then there's no worry that somehow that poet could make you less yourself and more another. Koch wasn't asking anyone to be imitative; rather, he was hoping that each of his students, by finding something inspiring in reading, would become inspired in writing, the inspiration leading to some kind of originality.

When I teach a class, I begin with a discussion of the theme or idea we're exploring, first by having the students talk about what they already know about it. I try to get a debate going, let people challenge each other a little, further develop their thinking. Only after this has happened will I give them the model poem we're going to look at. My idea is to show them that they already know things that the poem will talk about, and that they have opinions, and that they've drawn conclusions. If poet Juan Liscano (in chapter 3) has what seems to be a strange idea of "reality," finding it in the connection between silence and language, the students are ready, because of having already discussed "reality," both to entertain his point of view and to challenge it. Here's how one person has thought about this, I say, now what do you think? In this way, the poem with all its power cannot initimidate them; they already have their own authority.

Once we've discussed the poem, I ask the students to start writing. I try to frame this not as a directive (to write about dreams, loss, history, etc.). Rather, I ask the students to respond to the question or questions, the thoughts and ideas that the poem raises for them. I prefer not to dictate direction; if a student wants to go off in some odd way, I think that's fine, as long as it seems as if that inspiration has come out of the discussion or reading. A conversation about time (in chapter 1) that yields a poem about memory or dreaming makes sense to me. But a poem about fried chicken wings does not.

I sometimes put limitations on writing, depending on my knowledge of a student or group of students, but I do this only as a way of trying to open up the writing and make it deeper and more powerful. For example, in teaching dream poems (chapter 8), I've found it useful to refuse to allow students to write about nightmares because too frequently what I've received have been recitations of *Nightmare on Elm Street* plots. Other limitations I've imposed have been based on individual cases. Alex, a first grader who was quite a good writer, consistently wrote poetry about sports. As a sports fan myself, I understood his passion, but I felt his writing about it was limiting him, so I asked him not to include sports in his poems for a while. At first he balked, but then we negotiated. The first poem he wrote each week would not refer to sports, but if he had time to write another, the second one could. At first I worried that he'd race through the first poem to get to his sports poem and, in fact, the following week that was exactly what he tried to do. I didn't let him, though. I asked him to stay with the first poem a little longer, asking him questions,

9

getting him to reread and rethink what he'd written. Eventually, Alex began to spend more and more time with the first poem, becoming more and more interested in his own writing, to the point that he usually didn't have time to get to his second poem. Not that he stopped writing sports poems; he'd always have one to show me the following week. But he became a better writer and a better reader, I think, because of the demand I'd made of him, not simply to go beyond what he knew he already liked, but to go away from it completely and to places he'd never have considered if not pushed.

IV. Revision, Teachers & Writers, Books

One of the things I hope my students learn from me is to see how creative the process of revision can be. Too often, it's taught to them as a correcting process, a way of fixing "mistakes." Instead of seeing revision as an opportunity to question what they've written, to consider possibilities for what they've done, many young writers think about it as a neatening process, one in which the student can say, "Here, finished," and move on to something else.

To help other writers and teachers of writing offset this attitude, I discuss in this book some of the ways in which I teach revision. There are also two other sections that seem important to include. One is an appendix that describes a two-semester course I've taught for a number of years at Eugene Lang College, the undergraduate college at New School University (the former New School for Social Research), called the Teachers & Writers Collaborative Fieldcourse. It's both a writing and a teaching class in which we study the pedagogy of creative writing. As part of this study, during the second semester, in addition to their regular coursework, students work in the public schools as interns with writers from Teachers & Writers Collaborative.

Towards the end of this volume is a section on books. Our influences are an important part of how we write, teach, and learn. The books listed there are ones that have had an impact on my work both in the classroom and on the page. I include them as a quirky reference list and a possible inspiration, which other writers and readers may use as a point of departure.

Chapter 1

Three Lessons about Time

I. Trying to Figure It Out

Avenue of Time

there isn't a real story here
there's only the way
there are stars
reflected everywhere
to the ocean
the city
the sky
and they dance so crazy
in this reflection
it shows
how nothing in this universe
is fixed or forever
anything can happen
before the sun sets
or after
fortune and loss and change
striking
between the earth and stars

—*Mark Statman*

Time

Time goes everywhere around
the world
If time was backwards
the morning is night
and night is morning
and we sleep in the future

—*Jacob Cohen, first grade*

Over infinity, I said to a group of twelve fourth and fifth graders, scientists say that time and space are the same thing. I watched their faces. Thinking. Thinking. Then, enthusiastic responses.

Cool.

Star Trek.

Back to the Future.

Bubbling voices about Michael J. Fox, about Captains Kirk, Picard, and Janeway, deep space, time travel.

Except for one girl, a tremendously talented fifth grade writer. She didn't say anything, but her eyes took on a special glow. The other students had translated my comment into science fiction—their minds were watching movies. But she saw what the scientists saw. She got the idea of infinity and endlessness, the enormity of the universe. She saw the reason that time and space would have to be the same thing, that one was the other and that time and space, as we experience them in our daily lives, are not what, over eternity, they actually are. Time and space, as we know them, with their temporal dimensionality, are somehow false.

For a second, she glowed. Then she burst into tears, put her head down on her desk, and cried for almost an hour. I sat with her during much of that time, my hands on her shoulders, trying to comfort her, feeling vaguely guilty that what she had understood was my fault. Because she really *had* realized something. She'd not only understood the infinite, she'd understood, as children usually can't, the finite. And that knowledge was overwhelming. It had, she told me, frightened her. Which is normal. It echoes T. S. Eliot's lines in *The Four Quartets:*

Go, go, go, said the bird: human kind
Cannot bear very much reality.

To try to make sense of the hugeness of the universe is too hard. A leap of faith becomes necessary, one that allows us not only to acknowledge our inability to understand the logic of life but also to believe that there is one, as Einstein did when he noted that "God does not play dice with the universe."

Although the concept of time over infinity can be such a strange and difficult thing to understand, it isn't hard for children to understand time in the immediate. In a classroom, I demonstrate the idea of past, present, and future. I stand in front of a class and say, Look, in the future, I'm going to throw a piece of chalk in the air. Tell me when it is in the present. Then I throw the chalk. Present, the students shout. Now what is it, I ask. Past. I do this again. Show the chalk. Throw the chalk. Show it. Then I ask them if there is ever a point in which we are in the future? Ever a point when we are in the past? Is there ever a point when we are not living in the present?

Sometimes, I tell the students about how scientists have made the distinction between what they call space time and relative time. Space time is the big one: time over infinity. Space time refers to how the stars we see are so many light-years away, that what we're looking at in the night sky actually happened millions of years ago. Relative time is close. It's the one in which we can see ourselves living: personal history, family history, world history.

We always live in the present. Although that sounds obvious, it isn't something kids usually reflect on. They've been given so many ideas about time to think about through TV, movies, video games, books, and comics, that they don't think about time personally. Yes, they talk about wanting to be older, tell you what their careers might be or how they want to be older so that they can drive a car or live on their own. But for the most part they don't really wonder about time in their lives, how it passes, why it passes, what it means that time is infinite over infinity but finite in our lives. But a serious discussion gets them thinking about the meaning of time in their lives. How we can anticipate, want, wait, hope for the future. We can plan for it, imagine it, or wonder about it. But we can never be in it. Similarly, we can remember, retell, and even revise the past, but we can never be in it. In the largest sense of ego, we can never think about either past or future without thinking about ourselves because it is our "I" which is doing the thinking, imposing some kind of imagined or remembered order on whatever has been or will be.

II. Lesson One: What Does Time Do?

I begin this lesson by asking the students to think about time as they see it in their own lives. We talk about how they've seen themselves changing and growing. They often talk about how quickly they seem to change and how their parents never seem to change much at all and yet how they must be changing. We talk about the different ways time passes and the old cliché of how it flies when you're having fun and why they think it's true. Students are fascinated by the contrast between linear time and cyclical time (the way the seasons always return): everything gets older, but the world seems always to repeat itself.

Ciudad Maya comida para la selva

De la gran ciudad maya sobreviven
arcos
        desmanteladas construcciones
vencidas
          por la ferocidad de la maleza
En lo alto el cielo en que se ahogaron sus dioses

Las ruinas tienen
            el color de la arena
Parecen cuevas
            ahondadas en montañas
que ya no existen

De tanta vida que hubo aquí
de tanta
        grandeza derrumbada
sólo perduran
          las pasajeras flores que no cambian

    —*José Emilio Pacheco*

Mayan City: Food for the Forest

Of the great Mayan city the arches
survive
        ruined constructions
beaten
        by the ferocity of the weeds
High above is the sky where their gods drowned

The ruins have
          the color of sand
They seem like caves
           sunken in mountains
that no longer exist

Of all the life that once was here
of all

                    the grand collapse
              all that remains
                          are the unchanging passing flowers

When I teach Pacheco's poem—and I often do when I know a class has been studying great civilizations of the past—I point out how the poet looks at and describes time, and with it, nature. Over time, the once great city has become "ruined," "sunken," "collapsed." Nature is harsh here, the weeds are "ferocious," the sky even drowns the Mayan gods. We also talk about how the very appearance of the poem adds to this general effect. The uneven lines of the poem mirror the scattered remains of the city, spilling across and down the page, words like "survive" and "beaten" standing alone like smaller fragments among the larger ones.

In this poem, time is no friend to the Mayans. In fact, it seems to have been a companion destroyer with the human conquerors. Noting this, though, we also talk about how absent any humanity is from this poem. The only survivors are the flowers that, paradoxically, are both unchanging and passing. One sixth grader noted that Pacheco was describing a process that doesn't look like one: the flowers aren't always there, they just seem to be.

The Mayans never imagined the moment of this poem. To imagine it, they would not be able to include themselves. How could they see a world where they weren't? Who would be doing the seeing? The Mayan ruins are simultaneously a monument to the flourishing and the dying of a great civilization. For Mexicans today, the ruins are a source of pride because this greatness is part of their past, and thus this greatness is still in them. But what would the former inhabitants of the city say about what they would see today?

When the students write, I ask them to think about how time passes and changes their world. I remind them of the discussion we had, before reading the poem, about time in their own lives. What does it do to and for them? What do they think about all these things? Since time seems so constant, can they imagine a world beyond time, a place after time? I suggest, as they describe all these possible ideas and situations, to consider including how it makes them feel to be observing what they observe, to understand what they know. I can remember how happy fifth grader Luis Rivera looked as he catalogued the items he would leave in a box for a fifth grader of the future, the seriousness with which Tony Sheridan imagined and Jessica Laboy pondered the end of time. Mercedes Pimintel's description of time as being about love satisfies me because of how much I'd like to think it's true.

To the Fifth Grader Who Sits in My Seat

To the fifth grader who sits in my seat
30 years from now I leave in this box
my old sneakers and my fried chicken
one of my old pens and an old pencil
and my ring
my favorite food
Roy Rogers
my favorite candy
now and later
potato chips and my best toy
that I like, G.I. Joe
My color TV and my drawings too

Just for you
Thank you

   —Luis Rivera, fifth grade

After Time

After time you'll begin a new life as
another creature
and another creature will become you
After time the birds will stop singing

After time the fish won't swim
You won't play with your friends

After time the winds will end
After time the skies will end
And the waves won't smash
smash against the sand and
erode it away
That's what remains after time

   —Tony Sheridan, sixth grade

Walking thinking
about
how it was before
ruins

that people once lived
in
wondering if their spirits
are around
looking at what once
was alive
and what's alive
now
hoping that when
this
life is gone we
will be
history and hoping
that
other people would
study
our history which
was
once alive but which
will be in ruins

—*Jessica Lee Laboy, sixth grade*

Time changes and I grow up
and the world changes and
my mother grew old and
my teacher grew old too and
I still love my teacher in time
and time changes and
my teacher's dress is beautiful
Time is love
and time is beautiful like
my mom and my teacher
Time time time
It is time to stop writing
and I love just love
Time is a big heart

—*Mercedes Pimentel, fifth grade*

III. Lesson Two: Definitions of Time

In some classes I ask the kids to think about how to define time. It's surprisingly fun. Sometimes they point at the clock or the calendar as being what time is. So without clocks and calendars there'd be no time? I ask. Not exactly, they reply, and we get to the idea that these things measure time. So what is time? I refer to the poem fifth grader Mercedes Pimintel wrote in which she called time "love" and a "big heart." Sometimes I read them her poem. We talk about the beauty of the poem, lines like "I still love my teacher in time/and time changes and/my teacher's dress is beautiful," the wonderful juxtaposition of the teacher's dress and changing time which allows time to become so small and specific (the dress) and so large (the change) in the same moment in the poem.

For some students, though, Mercedes's description of time still seems too abstract. It's too much about feelings. So what, then? Days and nights? Our lives? History? But this is about people, I say. Does time need people? Is there time on Jupiter? Was there time in the days of the dinosaurs? Once, a third grader named Eric said that of course there was always time, but people were the only ones that paid any attention to it. Which led me to the question that if time is infinite, why are people always saying we're running out of it?

When we talk about time, I want the students to do some intellectual stretching on the subject. I want them to take what they're curious about and see how far they can go with it. I ask them to think about time in different ways. If it had a sound, a color, a voice, what would those be like? Who are the friends of time, who are the enemies? What would the dreams of time be like? What would time love or fear? These kinds of questions allow students to think imaginatively about an idea they may too often take for granted, to see it in another way, and to understand it more completely. I tell them about how Albert Einstein was able to understand light more completely by imagining that he was travelling with it, that he *was* it. I ask them to do the same kind of thing, to imagine that they are time. What would that be like?

When the students write, I prompt them to think about these different distinctions, definitions, and descriptions they've been making about time. I ask them to respond to their thinking, to write what they've been saying and see how far they can develop their ideas and descriptions. The students welcome this kind of exercise, with its mixing of science and poetry, facts meeting the imagination.

The rebirth of another occurs
You shrink into time
The memory of yourself becomes

less and less
Until there's no more
The days pass by
Like little violets in the
    Sunshine
But still life on earth begins
Another day passes the more time
    Begins
Night falls over the dawn
    And keeps going
The clock has no meaning
It just keeps track

    —*Lauren Loechner, sixth grade*

Time

People old people young time
doesn't care if it did we wouldn't
all live in this boring
world full of this hatred
world where time controls
night and day controls
hate and love
Time controls our minds that drift
in our minds
Time

    —*Norman Ayende, fifth grade*

Time goes all over the world
If time stopped, we would go
back into time and everything
would go backwards
People would, animals, things
that move
Schools would fall down
Lions would turn into cubs
Trees would turn into seeds
Bricks would get smaller and
smaller and crack
Day would go backwards
The world would be blank
and it would stop spinning
Everything would go backwards
by itself

Paint would disappear
So would everything
Food would come out of our mouths
People would turn into babies
When nothing is on this Earth
time will stop

    —Scott Roberts, first grade

This time
    it
still
    is
          the
    same
          the
          great
   yellow sun
          with
               the
               great
                    blue
               sky
                    you
                    can
               still
                    see
          the
               yellow and red

                    flower
         and if
             you look hard
you can still see the blue
ones
but
    the
    beautiful
          caterpillar
          is
               now
               a
               butterfly's
          cocoon
               that

<pre>
was
            made
was
            now
destroyed
with joy
the
            two
butterflies
fly away
</pre>

—Michael Armstrong, fifth grade

I like how sixth grader Lauren Loechner thinks about the time beyond "you" and the meaninglessness of clocks, and how first grader Scott Roberts writes about time stopping and everything going into reverse. Interestingly, relative time is a perspective that troubles Norman Ayende but reassures Michael Armstrong. But whether they are troubled or reassured, I think it's important for young people to be able to examine the ways they can see time. If they can do this, they can see that despite space-time's overwhelming hugeness, looking at relative time allows them to see time as something they can, if not control, at least try to understand and manage in their own lives.

IV. Lesson Three: The Meaning of the Future

Asking my students to imagine time often leads to discussions about political and social issues. It's easy to see why. Students are always studying current events, the environment, elections, negotiations. The headlines are about conflicts and poverty, about economic progress here, disaster there. Will there be a war somewhere? What does the President do? What is the Congress? What does social security mean? What is health care? What is the United States of America? What is the world?

Thinking about time helps students see how to connect these kinds of questions to their lives. When I ask them to think carefully about the past, present, and future, they naturally think about history, look at the present (this, *their* world), and wonder what the future holds for them. Will it be a good time? Sometimes they're very hopeful. We talk about what's good, what they have, what they dream of. We talk about how people are constantly trying to improve the world. The world seems politically safer, with fewer threats of world war, more attempts to negotiate peace. Scientists seem to be making major advances in technology and medicine. People are more aware of problems with the environment and are trying to do something about them. I remember one sixth grader in Harlem who told me about how his class had been studying environmental cleanup and who noted triumphantly how there are fish once again in the Hudson River.

But sometimes they're frightened. When I've asked them to write about how they feel about political and social issues, posing the questions, "What is it you want to say to America? What is it you want to say to the world?" their uncertainty about what is going on is clear. It isn't that they don't have joy in their lives, it's just that, given the chance to address their concerns about the world, they take the idea seriously. This seriousness leads to complex thinking that often leads to confusion. If things are getting better, they are also getting worse. There are fewer wars in the world, but many students have relatives in the armed forces still being sent to dangerous places. Violent crime may be decreasing but their experiences of it are often increasing.

Their list goes on. For every scientific advance, there seems to be a new disease. We're aware of the environment, but given global warming, the shrinking of the rain forests, the endangerment of so many animal and plant species, the students wonder if that awareness has come too late. Many of them live in poor neighborhoods. They see that there are more jobs, but there seems to be less security in those jobs. A booming stock market means little to them. In a world whose economy seems increasingly global and competitive, there's a sense that global doesn't mean communal and that for every winner in the competition, someone has to lose. They wonder how fair that is. A group of third graders told me that they had decided to stop buying certain products because they were made by exploited workers in China and Thailand. They felt that they were helping, they told me, but they also weren't sure if what they were doing was enough. Other times the students have referred to José Emilio Pacheco's "Ciudad Maya" and speculated about our cities, what they will look like when their present is the distant past. Examining time, what happens through it, because of it, with it, they had begun to wonder, as the African poet Keorapetse Kgositsile does in the poem below, what kind of ruins we will leave for the future and what we can do about it.

The Present Is a Dangerous Place to Live
(*excerpt*)

I. In the Mourning

And at the door of the eye
is the still voice of the land
· My father before my father
knew the uses of fire
My father before my father
was his multiple godhead,
sat on his circular stool
after the day was done. At times even
between the rednesses of two suns,
knowing that time was not born yesterday.
The circle continues
Time will always be
in spite of minutes that know no life.
Lives change in life
At times even rot
or be trampled underfoot
as the back of a slave.
There are cycles in the circle
I may even moan my deadness
or mourn your death,
in this sterile moment asking:
Where is the life we came to live?
Time will always be
Pastpresentfuture is always now
Where then is the life we came to live?

   —Keorapetse Kgositsile

America

America is dying
Bombs are flying, let us be
Free!!
    America, people
    are sighing, that's because
many are crying
    Why can't America
be free!
America = we want more
    but we
        don't give

          Back
Can
     America
          Take
               Back

Now one nation
stands at one. People
sad, many gone
     Only one nation

     —Kevin Costigliola, sixth grade

Raindrops of the Armageddon

The Lord has made a vow
never to flood the world again
but if the Lord sees that a lowly man
can break a promise
     what will happen then?
Will the rains come down in a torrent?
     Be warned, descendants of Cain, be warned.
Every chop at the tall oak wood brings us
     a
          rain-
               drop
                    closer
Every bullet shot at a fellow man brings us
     a
          rain-
               drop
                    closer
Every sin that is committed, every crime against nature
brings us a raindrop closer
closer to a sequel of the great Deluge
     Drop
          by
               Drop

     —Andy Martin, fifth grade

Death by Nuclear Air

Look! Look! Look!
At it! You can't
see it can't

you smell it
Look My God
I don't want to die
I don't want to die

   —*Awilda Gomez, seventh grade*

Possibilities of Life

The swiftness
of a tiger

how does it do a lash
of pain on
the earth
will the earth
die
in a different
universe, an explosion
swipes the galaxy
with fear, a possibility it will
run
run forever
to
the
unpossible
of
life

    —*Brenton Pennicooke, fourth grade*

Time

Once in our day
our world was quiet
Now in our days our
world is very bad
and violence is every
where and I wish
that one day we
could go back to
the past and make
everything quiet again
and clean

    —*Natalie DeJesus, fifth grade*

Time Is of the Essence

When I fall asleep
my eyes are opened
to a new light
On a different side
of the world
are they not doing

the same

    Is time a boundary
or is time just a tool
    a tool that tells us when
    we are going
        to wake up
    and to sleep

        Is life
worth living
        If we do not see new
    but just
    old
    monotonously repeated
    over
    and over
How can peace
    be found
when you won't
    try new
        things
    How can we look
at people
        as though
    they
    are
    puppets
        and we are the
puppet masters
        The show is
    about to begin

May you please take your seat

    —*Evan Lanoil, fifth grade*

Chapter 2

Origin, Family, Roots

I. Timelines: Public and Personal History

Angels (A Story)

When my grandmother died, I thought about angels. She came to me in a dream and said she would read my manuscript of poems. She promised to be honest and tell me which ones she liked and why. I asked her the difference between being alive and dying, of dying and being dead. She smiled and laughed and asked what difference did it make to me?

Later, I thought about how in the dream she looked as she had when I was eight or nine years old. We'd visit my grandparents almost every other weekend, either in Queens, where they lived, or they'd come out to Long Island to us. That was the time when we used to love her cooking, especially her chicken with dumplings. As she got older, it seemed like she lost something in her cooking, maybe a sense of proportion of spices. Meals she made were wonderful, but they were never as good as the memories of them.

I loved that time. It was fun to be a grandchild, to listen to stories about leaving Hungary, living in New York City, and growing up. The stories I liked most were the ones about how my grandparents met. She was holding a white kitten and he, by himself, he was lifting up a refrigerator under which the kitten had been trapped, he was that strong. My grandmother had thought he was the most beautiful man in the world. I liked to hear the one, too, about his white linen suit. She used to wash it every week so he could wear it on Sunday because he looked so good in it, walking down the street, a god in white. When he was a boy he met Babe Ruth twice, the Babe had waved at him, saying, Hey kid, how're you doing?

I think of my grandfather almost every day. I wonder vaguely if this means my grandparents are together now. My grandfather had blue eyes. Mine are blue but they're nothing like his. Mine are like clouds over the ocean. His were like the sky.

I look outside. The sky is gray to black in the middle of the day. The wind is blowing furiously, the trees are going crazy, and it looks like the thunderstorms from this morning are going to start again. A green and orange striped white paramedic truck is parked on the street and they're bringing someone out of the building across from ours on a stretcher. A woman holding a baby is crying.

In my dream, when I handed my grandmother my poems she started reading them without saying anything. I couldn't stand that and I woke up. It was still dark out and I just stayed there in bed, breathing and not thinking, not trying to go back to sleep.

—*Mark Statman*

Lineage

My grandmothers were strong.
They followed plows and bent to toil.
They moved through fields sowing seed.
They touched earth and grain grew.
They were full of sturdiness and singing.
My grandmothers were strong.

My grandmothers are full of memories
Smelling of soap and onions and wet clay
With veins rolling roughly over quick hands
They have many clean words to say.
My grandmothers were strong.
Why am I not as they?

—*Margaret Walker*

Lineage. Transpose the two syllables of that word. Age line. When I teach Margaret Walker's poem, I begin by asking my students what they know about their relatives who lived before them, about who they were and what they did. I ask them to think about how they might understand the connections between themselves and these people, some of whom they might not have even known. We talk about the stories they've been told from the past, why they think those stories are important to remember. In a classroom in the South Bronx, with thirty-three boys and girls clamoring to tell a story they'd been told, one fourth grader told me that telling these stories can help you understand who you are.

On the chalkboard, I draw a timeline and put Margaret Walker on it. I start with her birth in 1915. Then I go backward on the line and write in the grandmothers, grandfathers, a mother, a father. Then we go forward. I ask the kids to project, to invent children and grandchildren, filling in potential names and characteristics. They call these out, imagining the possibilities of Margaret Walker's life.

After we do this, we talk about how events in history affect people's lives on an individual level, about how who we are, what we're becoming, and where we are going are all connected to people before us. This is especially easy to demonstrate during times of international conflict—the Gulf War, events in Eastern Europe, for example—since a number of my students have had family in the military: reading the newspapers and watching the TV news, they knew who was going to fight and they were both worried and proud.

We go back to the poem and look at Margaret Walker's grandmothers, who were once slaves. She calls them strong. Margaret Walker is free. But what and where is her freedom, where does it come from? The Civil War only? This gets us talking about civil rights, about black people sitting in white restaurants, the fronts of buses, about marches in Selma, Montgomery, and Washington, D.C. We talk about people with visions of change. Often the kids mention stories their parents and grandparents, many of whom lived through these times, have told them, stories that show the impact of public history on private lives. Teachers often have a lot to add to this. Occasionally, visitors to the classroom can provide an interesting perspective on history. In one East Harlem fifth grade classroom, the teacher had her mother come to visit. Three classes crowded into one room, listened attentively, almost awestruck, as she dramatically described wars, the civil rights movement, the changes in the community, in all of New York, America, the world. The responses of the students were equally fascinating. They asked a lot of relevant questions, charmed by the half-historian, half-grandmother whose descriptions of their neighborhood's history inspired them to think in a new way about where they lived.

Having created a timeline for Margaret Walker and then having filled it with details of the time in which she lived, I ask the students to do their own. Sometimes I demonstrate by doing my own on the chalkboard. To show them how personal these can be, I include the usual things found in a conventional timeline—my birth, school, marriage, the birth of my son—as well as things that might not make a conventional timeline, but that do reflect what I think interesting or important to note about *my* life: the day of an epic bike ride, the time I broke my ribs, the day my son Jesse said "bunny rabbit," or the time I wrote an unusually satisfying poem. One event I include is the day I started working with this particular class.

Sometimes, when the teacher is willing, I ask him or her to make one of these lines as well, to compare and contrast with mine.

I ask the students to start with themselves and their families, and to try to connect all that to more public events. We put in presidential elections; sporting events (the World Series, the Super Bowl); and local, state, national, even world history (subway crime is down, the leaves are falling off the trees, more trouble or possible peace in the Middle East). Doing this becomes an interesting way for students to make connections with the world. Establishing for themselves that they too have a personal history that threads itself into a larger public one gives students a way to think about the relationship they have with the world.

Once they've plotted their timelines, I ask them to write poems inspired by them. I ask them to think about someone in their lives, from the present or the past, who means something to them and to find the words that they think best describe that person, the words with which they might want to praise that person. I remind them of how descriptive Margaret Walker's poem is, how much it appeals to the senses. In the first verse, we see the grandmothers far away, touching earth and (almost magically) making grain grow. We hear them singing. If the first verse gives us a kind of cinematic long shot of women far away, working in the fields, the second verse is a close-up. We are in the kitchen. We can hear their "clean words." We can even smell the grandmothers, the onions, and wet clay.

My Father

My father is my image.
My father is a part
of me. My father laughs
like the winds of the world.

My father smiles like the sun
like the light spreading
across the world,
that's my father.
My father is as handsome as
the moon and the morning
blue sky.

My father is as strong
as a storm and

as calm as
the sea.

—*Johnnel Mutunga, sixth grade*

When Matisca Sings

Oh dear girly hush
the dog
I'm trying to hear
Matisca sing

At 6:00 right on
the dot I listen to
Matisca sing

The alley cats don't mind
a bit we listen
to Matisca sing

Sing so sweet knock
the socks off me

I love it
when Matisca
sings

—*Tamara Simpkins, fifth grade*

The Secret Planet

My mom is a rose in the secret planet and
I am a rose, too

On my birthday
I was a music book

—*Marisol Alejandro, third grade*

In these poems, there is a great deal of Walker's kind of describing. Johnnel Mutunga gives us his father's image, his laughter, smile, and strength. Tamara Simpkins describes how everything has to stop so she can hear her neighbor singing. Marisol Alejandro finds herself on a secret planet where you and those you love are able to become the things that you love.

II. Hidden Craziness, Knowing Ourselves

Jesse (28 October 1993)

we waited for you
for so long
we didn't know anything

now you're home

— *Mark Statman*

Sometimes when I teach Margaret Walker's "Lineage," I compare her timeline to a family tree. Usually the older students are familiar with how to draw one. Although there are different ways to draw a family tree, the one I've seen them do most often puts the great-grandparents at the top of the tree, then grandparents, then the parents, and then at the base of the tree, at the roots even, they place themselves. But when they compare the tree to a timeline, they find the tree isn't as satisfying for them. The kids will note that the tree is, in fact, misleading because it ends with the child on the bottom. Which would make the child the root. But a child is not a root. In Walker's poem, the grandmothers have rooted the poet with their strength and love.

Lucille Clifton's poem "roots" attempts to connect what is essential in the past to what is essential in the present by naming it.

roots

call it our craziness even,
call it anything.
it is the life thing in us
that will not let us die.
even in death's hand
we fold the fingers up
and call them greens and
grow on them,
we hum them and make music.
call it our wildness then,
we are lost from the field
of flowers, we become
a field of flowers.
call it our craziness
our wildness
call it our roots,

> it is the light in us
> it is the light of us
> it is the light, call it
> whatever you have to,
> call it anything.

My students are often initially quite puzzled by the poem—what is she talking about? What does she mean "the light," what does she mean about death, what is this thing of becoming the field? It's odd: the language of the poem is easy, direct, so *simple*. Students wonder why something that reads so easily is so hard to understand.

To help them, I ask the students to think about themselves. What makes each one of you who you are? I ask. What makes you different, not just from the person sitting next to you, but different from the person you've been? They find it easy to talk about this: physical growth, personality development. But I then ask: What makes you the *same* person now that you were five years ago, ten years ago? What makes you the person you've *always* been?

For many, these are odd questions because this kind of self-analysis or critical consciousness is unfamiliar and difficult terrain. They note certain kinds of things: I've always liked pizza but I haven't always liked basketball, before I just liked to run; I couldn't read before, but I always liked it when someone read me books; I used to like *Sesame Street* but now I prefer horror films. But they quickly see that none of these things, not basketball, pizza, running, books, nor television, while significant, is essential to their lives. But the initial thinking about such things can help them, through deeper analytical thinking, into seeing other, more essential sides of themselves: they can figure out that playing basketball and running demonstrate a desire for movement, play with others, friendships. Liking pizza tells them about the pleasure they can find in certain foods. Television and books, whether read by or to them suggest a growing desire to learn and to imagine. The very fact that they are changing often leads them to conclude that change itself is a necessary constant. As we continue to talk about the important things in their lives and figure out why those things have meaning, the students are able to see much more clearly the whys behind what they know about themselves; they are able to see constants in their thoughts and emotions, in their creating and dreaming.

Sometimes the discussion ventures into notions of the spirit and the spiritual. Students get the connection between the spirit (sometimes they call it the soul) and Clifton's "light," the "life thing in us / that will not let us die." We contrast this with her image of "death's hand," noting that, if Clifton is right, if we cannot die, then death is not something to be afraid of. The hand might extend itself, but we can fold its fingers up and take control of death. The green that death becomes is about renewal, the humming is about joy. For Clifton, the life thing that is in us, that *is* us, the craziness and wildness, is so powerful that even when we think we are lost, it's only a matter of perspective. You are not lost from the field if you allow yourself to become part of it because, as part of the field, you'll know exactly where you are (I think of Wallace Stevens's idea that to understand the snow and ice we must have a "mind of winter").

Finally, I ask my students why the poem is called "roots." Their answers vary but they are all related to a single idea—that roots nourish us, keep us grounded, allow us to live. The craziness Clifton speaks of in the poem is not madness, but fearless excitement, willful ecstasy. Being rooted in the earth means that craziness and wildness need not be aimless and destructive because, as with the "we" and "our" of the poem, Clifton means they are part of one's history, family, and community.

Before my students begin to write, I sometimes read them another Lucille Clifton poem, "new bones":

new bones

we will wear
new bones again.
we will leave
these rainy days,
break out through
another mouth
into sun and honey time.
worlds buzz over us like bees,
we be splendid in new bones.
other people think they know
how long life is
how strong life is.
we know.

To begin a discussion, I talk about Clifton's certainty that there are things others may think they know, but which we *know* we know. I ask them to think about things in life that seem absolutely real and certain to them and to think how that certainty might give them "roots"—just as Clifton's confidence comes from her own sense of that inner light. What would they call their roots? What is their light? What runs with them, sings with them, in them? I ask them to think about their own ideas of what is possible for the world and for them.

> I woke up in the country of
> North Carolina and the golden green grass
> was my bed. The golden sun is my
> lamp. And I live in the forest.
> It is my home. It is a place of
> warmth. It is a beautiful place.
> It is a forest with golden trees,
> with leaves made of emeralds and the
> roses are as red as rubies.
> I live in these woods. I am these
> woods. The North Carolina woods.
>
>   *—Vincent Blakely, fourth grade*

The Words inside Me

> The
> words in
> side me describe
> the way I act.
> When something scares me
> I show fear.
> My dark half tells me to be
> mad and ferocious.
> My good half shows love and
> care.
> So you see these words tell
> me how to act.
>
>   *—Theo Washington, fourth grade*

Call Me

> Call me sweet
> call me friendly
> call me pretty
> but do not call
> me ugly

35

because you will
see me get ugly
very ugly and you will
not want to see me
again

   —Sophia Negron, fifth grade

Call it our funniest even,
call it the world
it is the universe thing in us
that lives
Even in my hands
I fold my fingers up
and call them purple and
grow on them which makes rap
call it our dumbest then
we are lost from the meadow
of roses we become
a meadow of flowers
call it our greatest
our funniest
call it our words
it is the dark in us
it is the dark of us
it is the dark, call it
whatever you want to,
call it the universe.

   —Rabina Greene, fifth grade

I am born as I get
to see nature
flowers blooming I nature
is in my hand
as I see the
earth start
to
spin as I feel it in my
soul as I admire myself as it is
a picture of myself as
I am going to live or
die as
I feel the sun bursting

on me as I am myself
I start
to
grow as God is
talking to me don't
fear if death
I am
here
with you
As I talk to
myself
I feel in my blood as
I feel healthy not sick
as nature is
blowing away until I
listen to what
they are
saying as
beams feel
like they
are taking me to heaven
or hell as I get scared
I feel haunted but
I get a family. As
I feel in my mind
as I sing to myself
as I celebrate because
I had parents
as it never ends
as it shines
to heaven as
there is no such
thing as hell as they bring me
for as my soul stays gold as
God stays I am myself

   —Chris DeMeglio, sixth grade

I have sunshine each and every day
    but as I focus out my window
        sick from the cold weather
I can feel my solemn soul
    translating through my body
    a tear falls from my dark
        brown eyes

When I start to cry my fulfilling
  angels tell me to fulfill
    my happiness

—*Erica Hardaway, fifth grade*

These young poets name their roots in many ways. Vincent Blakely's are in the woods of North Carolina, where he feels connected and happy, at home. Theo Washington's words inside him describe a conflict within himself, a conflict about what his language does and that he struggles to understand. Sophia Negron also connects roots to the power of language, but she refers to the power of words to change things, to be both mystical and practical. Rabina Greene is inspired by Clifton in a different way. She's influenced by Clifton's form, but is unsure of the content. The present, she told me, isn't so great that you can just say everything is fine. And she wondered, too, about the future. A gifted young writer and an interesting thinker, she didn't really believe her life was going to get much better.* This perspective is not shared by some of the other poets: Chris DeMeglio and Erica Hardaway, even as they thought about what's wrong with the world, responded to the problems of their lives like Clifton, with faith and hope.

---

* An important point here: whatever Rabina believes about her life, she's also written a good poem. Good poems often come out of disappointment or unhappiness. A lot of times, teachers will worry that their students' poems are too unhappy. They'll want to *disagree* with the poet about the ideas or emotions of the poem, which doesn't seem to me to be a useful critical stance. It wrongly suggests that there are correct and incorrect things a poem can be about, that certain emotions are acceptable, while others are not.

Chapter 3

It's Real for Me but Not for You So Now What?

I. The Problem: What We Know

question

small hand at the light
over the light
through the light
hand
off the light
the gesture of yes and no
becoming the same
it was
"I thought I told you yesterday" and the looking back
in memory becomes
a looking back *for*
yesterday and the conversation
one person had and the other
didn't
as though language is
something predictable
like the ocean has waves
the sky a sun
what chance is there of
going through life like
a dream and then not knowing
if you had this talk before
not waking up because
the clock isn't ringing
there is never a sound
no matter how carefully you listen

—*Mark Statman*

In My Perfect World

In my perfect world, God
is the head. There are many animals
in the world. They are playing
with each other.
Look at the lion dancing with the
cat. Another cat came over and
they are spinning me around.
In my perfect world, there are
butterflies and birds and animals
and the animals are friendly to
you.

—Romel Wilson, second grade

I worry a lot about the world kids live in today and the world that my generation is making for them. I worry about the things kids know and the things they don't know. I'm not talking here about preserving innocence, or arguing that knowledge is wrong. But I am concerned that they don't always know the meaning of their knowledge. For example, they know AIDS kills, but conversations with young people about dying reveal what an abstraction it is to them: a fourth grader, comparing it to a video game, told me he'd just get up and live again. Their ideas about right and wrong also have a similar kind of abstraction. When I talked with a group of fifth graders about the emotional, intellectual, and physical violence of racism and sexism, they gave as examples some popular television shows, noting that they knew what was going on was wrong. But many of them felt that as long as the presentations of these kinds of behaviors were funny, it was all right for the characters to treat each other with intolerance and cruelty.

The problem is that the images children are exposed to through all the various communications media—images that offer a model for what to want and how to act—are not always the images they see outside their windows. Too many times students have told me about the "fact" of time travel, the existence of intergalactic wars, and of superheroes, believing in these things simply because they've seen them on television. And even if the media don't necessarily tell us what to think, they do tell us what to think about. Television, movies, music, and magazines offer images of what's valuable, desirable, hip, or important. These images are not a description of how the world is; rather, they are a means for advertisers to encourage kids to participate in a consumer society. As such, the differences between the worlds kids live in and the worlds they're taught to desire create a serious communication problem that can cause a desperate confusion that children long to have resolved.

One of the things I hope to do with my students is to help them see how they can resolve this confusion. I do this by asking them to write about what they think they know and understand about their reality and to see how to make sense of it. For example, I read Romel Wilson's poem and look at what he thinks perfection is: order, play, community, beauty. That is to say, a world he doesn't experience. I look at Daniel Cohen's poem below and I see what he does experience:

Reality—Something We Don't Even Want

Reality
is a sun shining day ruined
by a
thunderstorm
Reality
is three errors
in the
bottom of
the ninth
Reality
is
beginning
to mean nothing
Reality
is
milk with orange juice
Reality is a cupcake
with no icing
Reality
is oranges
I hate oranges
Why
do I hate
oranges
Because
of
the taste
Taste
is reality

Reality is
a hand
with no fingers
Reality
is
a hand
offering me oranges

These poems were written by children who are very different. Romel is an African American living in one of the poorest neighborhoods in the United States, Mott Haven in the South Bronx. Daniel is a white sixth grader from suburban Long Island. But both write about a world that seems essentially hostile. Romel wants the intervention of God to create order. Daniel is constantly forced to face that what he doesn't want is what is happening.

I spend a lot of time asking kids to think about how they understand reality. It's something I've watched a lot of good teachers do—to assume that the classroom is not the starting point and ending point for how and where learning happens. These teachers know how to take the material of the classroom—history, science, literature, whatever—and compare and contrast it to the world (or worlds) their students live in and do or do not understand. And they do this at every level, from pre-K to college.

As a teacher of writing, I know that asking students to think about all the different ways of thinking about reality is another way to get them writing. It presents them with new ways of thinking about perspective—their own and those of others—and opens them up to the question of what's real for whom and why. Writing about reality, how they understand it, and then listening to what others have to say about it gives them a sense of the importance of accepting difference, just as it shows them what's common in those experiences. As Neal Postman notes in *The End of Education*, one of the most important things we need to do in teaching children is not only to improve their self-respect, but to teach them to respect the selves of those around them. Letting the kids do their own exploring lets them see that their realities, their ideas of order (and disorder) are neither abstract nor arbitrary. It lets them face themselves, as well as others, and in so doing, they are able to identify the experiences they have that are unique and the experiences that they have that are common, a vision not only of the self but the community.

II. The Lesson: Be Quiet

When beginning any discussion of reality, I usually ask the students to talk about how they know that something is true, how, when presented with information, they can be sure that what they're hearing is accurate. For this discussion, we talk about direct experience as well as indirect experience. If I tell them a story and someone contradicts it, how would they figure out who was telling the truth?

I tell them about the time my friend Joe and I went mountain biking and when we came to a fork in the road that was the beginning and end of a trail loop, Joe decided to go one way and I decided to go another. I tell the students that when we passed each other he warned me about a rattlesnake he'd seen on the trail. But when I got to the place where he'd seen the snake, I saw a long stick that, in fact, did look like a rattlesnake. So, I ask my students, what was it, a snake or a stick? A stick, they say. But what does Joe think, I ask. Well, they argue, he thinks it's a snake but he's wrong. Here, we're getting at the difference between truth and reality, I tell them. For Joe, the truth is that he saw a snake. He wouldn't be lying to anyone if he told them he'd seen a rattler. This bothers the students a little bit because they think that since they know what really happened, Joe can't possibly believe otherwise. Except, I remind them, the only reason they think they know what happened is because they trust me. How, in fact, do they know that I'm not lying? Or how do they know that there wasn't, in fact, both a snake and a stick there and that the snake left before I got there?

Now the students understand the point of our discussion: by not having directly experienced what happened, their version of it came from an indirect experience of it, through me. They could accept that version as "real" or not, depending on how much they'd decided to trust me. In some classes, I've asked them what they'd think if they found out I'd made the whole story up for the sake of the lesson. And would it make a difference if I had made it up? This question sometimes confuses them, the idea of the truth in the made-up story, but eventually they see the point: their sense of reality is a combination of direct and indirect experiences, and how much they trust those two will determine their sense of reality.

We talk about other ways to think about reality. I ask them to think about the difference between the reality of science versus the reality of religion. We talk about how even though we perceive the world with our senses (for example, they can tell what they will have for lunch by the smells from the cafeteria), how we interpret our sensory perceptions is often determined by prior interpretations and values (that they know what they're having for lunch doesn't mean they'll want to eat it). In *Pedagogy of the Oppressed*, the great Brazilian educator Paolo Freire tells of showing a photo to some tenement residents in Santiago, Chile. The photo shows a group of men standing on a street corner with another man off to the side getting drunk. The photo is supposed to be about the evils of drinking. But the men Freire shows it to see it quite differently. Their interpretation is that the men on the corner are lazy and unemployed, while the drunk man is a real worker who, with money to spare, is taking a deserved break from his labor.

La Realidad es ahí donde el silencio . . .

La realidad es ahí donde el silencio
propicia el nacimiento del lenguaje.
Porque antes que el oído están los ruidos
y antes que la vista lo creado
y antes que las palabras están las cosas.
Callar para poder mirar oír y hablar
en una lenta floración olvidada.

　　—*Juan Liscano*

Reality is there where the silence . . .

Reality is there where the silence
means the birth of language.
Because before something is heard, there is noise
and before something is seen, it's created
and before there are words, there are things.
Be quiet, so you can see, hear, and speak
in a slow flowering of forgetfulness.

When reading this poem by Venezuelan poet Juan Liscano, the students and I talk about how, for Liscano, having an experience and then being able to name that experience is how the poet understands reality. We talk about his idea, too, that something has to have happened before we can name it. Some students have said you can imagine something that isn't real and describe it, but others have countered that that doesn't necessarily make what you've imagined real.

The last two lines are often a real puzzler for the students, in part because of their abstractness. I try to explain the lines in the context of what Liscano is asking. He wants us to be quiet, to notice. But he doesn't want us to notice what we already know. He wants us to see and hear and say what we normally wouldn't, to look at a world that always has been there but that we have forgotten to pay attention to.

Finally, as they read the poem, I ask the kids to pay attention to how Liscano has written it. I ask them to note the repetitions, in particular, the way in which the repetition of the word *before* creates a tight rhythmic build-up that contrasts strongly with the relaxed flow of the closing lines.

For some of my students, though, Liscano's faith in language and experience are not enough. In part, it's because their age has given them neither enough language nor enough experience to gauge how they understand the world. They're forced to rely on the experiences of others, what their parents tell them, what they learn in school, what they get from the media. But with so many different sources, the reality they receive is a fragmented one. And the received realities are ones they don't have the maturity or the experience to assess analytically. And so, the students don't question the validity of what they've experienced; what they do question is the conflict between their experiences and the experiences of others: this is real for me for now, but it isn't for someone else, so what is it? As they begin their writing, I suggest that they think about that question. I ask them to think about how they understand how the question of different experiences and interpretations appears in their own lives, reminding them of how it happened for me and my friend Joe. I reread Liscano's poem to them, asking them to think about how for this poet language is at the heart of reality. Finally, I urge them to try to follow his final instructions: to be quiet, so they can see, hear, speak.

Did It Really Happen?

Wind, you can feel it, but you don't
You can sing, but you don't
You can read a great book, but you don't
You can have a conversation, but you don't
You can walk, but you don't
You can know someone, but you don't
You can do all these things
but if you don't remember them
You never really did them

—*Gayle Wayne, fifth grade*

Reality

You need silence to make reality
Reality can be a clock
Reality can't be a time machine
The start of a clock is silence
Then you build it
A time machine does not need silence
It is not reality
You can find reality wherever you go
Go ahead
Sit on a rock in the woods
Reality is the long, thin, green grass
Reality is the rustling leaves on the
tall, brown trees
Reality is the small, white, furry bunnies
Reality is people
and Reality is you

    —Desiree Raffi, fifth grade

I was walking in the
street I saw this ugly tree with
no leaves and green branches

I saw this car riding
with no wheels and no windows
no doors and also no chair

    —Rodrigo Murillo, sixth grade

What is Reality?
Life formed on Earth
Does it exist with the energy of space?
Yes, no, maybe so
No one will ever know

Why are flowers used as a person's name?
Is it because they're beautiful and
have attraction
Do you think it's because they feel like it?

What is up in space?
Gases and features only?
They work in a special way

The sun as a light bulb, the stars as
fireflies, and the sky as blueberry juice

Does it exist at all?

   —*Rose Garcia, sixth grade*

Is Reality Stone?

   New York, dark, gloomy buildings
Connecticut, light grassy houses
   New York Reality, Connecticut
fantasy. Which is Reality? We don't know. It's
just a building or a house to us. Where do we come
from, Connecticut or New York, fantasy or reality?
We're trapped in buildings every day, not knowing.
Is reality stone? Is reality stone? Is Reality
like Medusa, inside dark and gloomy, and then
outside, just a block of stone?
   Who knows? Do you?

   Is Reality stone?

   —*Jerry Medina, Jr., sixth grade*

What is air?
What are people?
You can see evil, speak evil, or hear evil if
we don't have language, eyes, or ears.
What is the meaning of love? Is it blind?
Is there life after death?
Why do I write this poem?
Do I have a life?
Do I have a love?
Am I something in a big blue ball that spins
in a big black place?

   —*Joshua Nuñez, sixth grade*

The City of New York

In the city I see
many people getting hurt in many ways
seeing people mugging others' valuables

Homeless people on the streets
looking around for little scraps of food
Singing the song "Akuna Matata"

Words which mean no worries
I hear many different sounds in NY
such as many gunshots everywhere

Going from drugs to heads
sniffing up the drugs to their noses
No, not afraid to die

    —Jason Petrone, sixth grade

What Is Reality?

Is reality round?
Or is it things that have
been seen, heard, and spoken
about?
Why is Rose a person and
has not just been kept
as the name of the flower?

Why do I sit next to
Rose and not a flower?

Why are roses red and not
green or blue, the colors I like?

Now tell me, if what I just
wrote is reality
    is it?

    —Zoraida Jasmin Rivera, sixth grade

I Don't Believe in Complete Reality

I don't believe in complete reality
After everything dies, it is reborn
but not completely

But with the partial reality there is
too much taken for granted

The trees that I climb in the backyard
what comes between the seasons

how people's clothes fit
how you will never ever see the same cloud twice

and where does it go . . .
why does it leave
why is so much taken for granted
and would it be better
if we knew
and why don't we realize how much this world
has to offer
do we even notice, or care

    —Sari Zeidler, fifth grade

The variety of the resulting poems is extraordinary. For some of the students, like Gayle Wayne, reality is connected to memory. If two people share an experience and only one person remembers it, then the experience was real only for the one person. For the other, it's as though it never happened. Other students—Rose Garcia, Jerry Medina, Jr. and Zoraida Jasmin Rivera, for example—think about reality as an issue of trust, and their poems reflect this as they question the world around them. Desiree Raffi sees reality as something we actively look for. It's as though we perceive reality by acting through it, or creating it; the world is there only because we notice it, what we don't notice doesn't count. Sari Zeidler and Rodrigo Murillo have much grimmer perspectives on reality; they look at it passively, wondering why anyone bothers to think experiencing this world makes any difference at all.

Chapter 4

Silence

I. The First Time I Heard Silence

lost hearts

I know about lifting
the covers off my thinking
or about trying to imagine
that in the morning
whatever wasn't all right last night
will be
the way there's always
a morning and sun
to replace the night and moon
it's possible to cry
about what I can't remember
and even more possible
to stop moving anywhere
it's like people repeating their names
over and over
as though waiting for someone else
to change the subject
now let's talk about
what we believe in
a silence so long
everyone looks up
to see what happened

—*Mark Statman*

In Oaxaca, Mexico, the orange flower city, and in the ruins outside it at Yagul and Dainzu, I consciously began to hear silence for the first time. It's not that there wasn't sound, but there were moments, late at night, early morning, when the background of silence became the most practical and exotic way to hear sound. It was every sharp clop of a burro's hooves on cobblestone, every radio voice, soft sweet guitar strums lingering and wavering through the air. It was sitting on a hill where a Zapotec temple once had been, site of human sacrifice, and looking out over the green valley, hearing the lowing of cows and the bleating of sheep, the voices of the herders and of farmers with machetes cutting corn. And this listening, it wasn't the case of one sound layering over another sound. It was a sound heard clearly against what at first thought seemed like nothing at all. Only silence, I was beginning to understand, isn't nothing. It only seems to be when compared with the idea of listening and hearing as the distinguishing, labelling, and ordering of various sounds, some fully allowed, others partly filtered, others blocked by the brain.

Since that time in Oaxaca, I've found myself able to notice silence everywhere, from summer nights on a stoop in Brooklyn to late evening fishing on the Cow Pasture River in western Virginia, wading through the slow, cool water. I've heard it on beaches and subway platforms, in snow, in rain, in wind. When you hear silence, it has a remarkable presence, a way of leading the listener beyond noise and language. It leads to a kind of listening that *seems* passive because it is neither critical nor interpretive. Hearing silence is about letting the sounds of the world come to you. It is about stopping and not doing, giving yourself a chance to hear things not only as you want them to be or assume them to be or think they may be. It is about learning to eliminate the identity of the "listener" from the equation and to hear things as they are.

II. Silence as Presence

Hay silencio en la lluvia

hay silencio en la lluvia que cae estripitosamente sobre
el techo de lámina
en nuestro pensamiento hay silencio
en medio del ruido externo a veces estamos sumergidos en
el más profundo silencio y cuando de pronto un sonido
nos arranca de nuestra quietud se nos hace insoportable
toda voz y todo lo que nos llama nos rompe
sin embargo a veces rodeados de silencio parecemos estar
llenos de ruido los pensamientos suenan las manos suenan
al aire crepita y el más dulce rostro es altisonante
    el espacio se vuelve una enorme caja de resonancia
donde golpea sin cesar el tiempo, pero también ocurre

que al hablar la voz no suena aunque lo pensado
parece arañar los vidrios

   —*Homero Aridjis*

There's Silence in the Rain

there's silence in the rain that falls crashing on
the tin roof
in our thoughts, there's silence
in the middle of all the noise around us, sometimes we're
    submerged in
the deepest silence and when suddenly a sound
drags us from our quiet every voice
becomes unbearable and everything that calls us breaks us
sometimes, surrounded by silence, we seem to be
filled with noise, our thoughts sound, our hands sound
the air crackles and the sweetest face sings too high
      space becomes a huge box of sound
where time beats without stopping, where, at the same time
the voice talking makes no sound though what's thought
seems to scratch at the windows

Al Silencio

Oh voz, única voz: todo el hueco del mar,
todo el hueco del mar no bastaría
todo el hueco del cielo,
todo la cavidad de la hermosura
no bastaría para contenerte,
y aunque el hombre callara y este mundo se hundiera
oh majestad, tú nunca,
tú nunca cesarías de estar en todas partes,
porque te sobra el tiempo y el ser, única voz,
porque estás y no estás, y casi eres mi Dios,
y casi eres mi padre cuando estoy más oscuro.

   —*Gonzalo Rojas*

To Silence

Oh voice, only voice: not all of the ocean's emptiness,
not all of the ocean's emptiness is enough
not all of the sky's emptiness,
nor the hollowness of beauty
is enough to hold you,
and even though a man becomes quiet and this world disappears

oh power, you never
you never will stop being everywhere
because you are greater than time and existence, only voice,
because you are and you aren't, and you're almost my God,
and you're almost my father when I'm at my darkest.

In Juan Liscano's poem (in chapter 3), silence becomes the moment before reality begins. Here, for Gonzalo Rojas, silence is not a moment before; rather, it is the source of his voice, as a poet and as a human being. Silence is the space in which the universe resides. In Homero Aridjis's experience, as well as my own, silence is inherent in all things that make sound; sound and silence exist because of each other.

The value of being aware of the presence of silence amidst the noise of our lives is one that seems to be disappearing from my life, and I wonder if this isn't true for a lot of people. Living in a city should not make it harder to do that kind of listening. That there are noises should, in fact, call attention to our need for silence, for taking moments to stop and rest and hear the world.

But often what I've observed is that what people do to get away from the noises of the city is to add more noises to it. They speak over others (who cares what they're saying?). They lean hard on their car horns (who cares if the light has only just changed?). They make it so loud that the next person has to become louder in an exponential explosion of useless volume.

Sometimes, and I wonder if this isn't worse, I've dealt with noise by cutting myself off from it, the way a few seconds ago I closed the window, not because of the cold but because there was someone shouting as he walked down the street. I didn't take the time to find out why, nor did it occur to me that I wouldn't hear it anymore once he moved off the block. I closed the window. I stopped trying to hear and understand what is out there, both in its sound and in its silence. And this can happen anytime, anywhere. At that moment, I've actively, willingly, *willfully* given up something valuable. Losing the silence of the world also means losing something of the sounds of the world because of how much avoidance goes into my listening. It's harder to walk down the street the way Whitman does in *Leaves of Grass* and to notice the sounds of that street, the voices, music, traffic, the urban energy. I've practiced not noticing so much that I have to remind myself to stop, to follow Liscano's admonition to be quiet and to hear the old, familiar sounds or the new and resonant ones.

III. A Lesson in Silence

There are a number of different ways in which I've asked students to think about silence. With kindergartners and first graders I've done it by asking them to make sounds: the sound of a train, a truck, a car, a plane. What's the sound of the wind, the wind in the trees, the ocean? And then I ask them for the sound of silence. Not a movement in the class, not a sound. Is it completely silent? Of course not. But by contrasting the sudden quiet with the sounds they've just been making, we get pretty close.

With older kids, I start by asking them to notice sound and silence away from the classroom. Anticipating that this is what we'll talk about in the following session together, I give them the assignment of taking some time over the following days to listen. Listen in the street. Listen at home at night in bed. Listen to the morning. Then, during our next time together I ask them to tell me the different things they noticed. We talk about why some things are more noticeable than others. One of the things they always seem to pick up on is how relative volume is: that a cat can seem louder than a truck if the cat is all that's there and all you want to do is sleep, whereas the truck in the middle of the day is something you can barely hear over the sound of the subway train—in fact, you might not notice it at all.

After talking all this through, I ask them now to be not as quiet as they can, but as *silent* as they can. We try it several times until we're all satisfied with our level of silence. Then I ask them to think about what happens when the silence happens. How does it make them feel? What does it make them think about? I ask them to think about how sound compares with silence—are they part of each other or separate? Does one contain the other? We think about how physical silence can feel, how essential it can be in our lives. Then, with all these ideas floating around, I ask them to write.

Stumped

Writing for Mark one sunny day
    like this
It's hard to think of something to write
    Ah ha!
I've thought and I finally have it
    it's a beautiful
poem and a beautiful day for it too

I will read it to my
        class
to make their eyes shine like golden suns
        This is my poem for
        Mark
        Silence
Silence sweet silence
        no trains no buses
        no babies crying
        no people arguing
        no wars
Nothing but sweet silence and peace

    —*Lauryn Bermudez, fifth grade*

Early in the Morning

Early in the morning
before the sun shall rise
a quietness, a stillness
shall come before your eyes
and the only sounds that can
be heard are the sounds the
stillness cries
The sound of water
of water silent rippling
to the bank
the sound of sea gulls calling
to each other from
a distance, the sound of
rushes rustling and
whistling in the wind
a quietness, a stillness

    —*Edrid Sanabria, fourth grade*

De noche

De noche se oye el sonido
de las olas aullando
las estrellas brillan en el cielo
y las olas del mar chocan
contra las piedras
De repente
los arboles se remecia
asustado abri mis ojos
mire por todos lados

no
vi
nada
ni siquiera el mar
   —Luis Chavez, fifth grade

At Night

At night one hears the sound
of the waves howling
the stars shine in the sky
and the waves of the ocean beat
against the stones
Suddenly
the trees sway
Frightened, I opened my eyes
looking all around
I saw
nothing
not even the ocean

Chapter 5

Loss

I. A Story

Talking with students about loss is complicated, often difficult, sometimes unavoidable, and at times necessary. The students know about losing a toy, a game, or an argument. They know about friends' moving from the neighborhood or about moving away themselves. They know about pets that become lost or that die. They know about the deaths of people they've loved. I've found that students often want to talk and write about these kinds of things. They're interested in wondering about loss, the sense and senselessness of it, how strange and hard it is when someone or something is gone. I feel close to this kind of wondering. It's very much a part of my own writing.

Some Losses I Want to Acknowledge

> *How could I have come so far?*
> *(And always on such dark trails!)*
> *I must have travelled by the light*
> *Shining from the faces of all those I have loved.*

—Thomas McGrath

Space filling time, space becoming time, space as conjunction and conjecture, time as days I haven't thought about or worried about or dreamed the way dreaming is myth-making, an activity for the future, a puzzle, not a problem, a space uninvited, unified, and longed for. Put on your hat. Go outside. But *really* outside. Go where you haven't been in so long there aren't any maps anymore.

Alta's shadow falls across the snow. She holds a Bible. She doesn't open it. Are you listening to me? Her lips move the words. No sound. So cold in the wind. Can you fall into the snow? Move your arms? Now I'm an angel, she thinks. All the angels. She knows the word *demon*. God is a demon, she thinks. Then she takes it back, afraid that God has been in her thoughts and heard her. God fights the demons. She says it. That's why he has angels. To sing songs and to fight for him.

Alta's sisters aren't anywhere. When she went looking for them, the snow had just started. But it was such a fast snow that by the time she got to where her shadow now fell, there was too much snow and her sisters were all gone. I can't take care of them, she thought. I can't do this anymore. It makes no difference how much you love them. She turns and walks away, realizing the whole time, she doesn't know where she's going, knows only nowhere.

What I'm afraid of too many times comes true. Two days later, when I went looking for Alta, no one could tell me where she was. A year later, it seemed like no one even knew who she was. She should be thirteen years old. I met her when she was six, I walked into her classroom and she looked up at me shyly and told me about her little sisters and a pet rabbit. Her copper face was glowing and she reminded me of a Caribbean sun that I slept under on a beach, as happy in my life as I've ever been. I've known her for so many years, read her poems, watched her grow. How can no one know where she is?

I have these dreams full of anger. They fill the night, these angry colors, red, black, red, black, and I scream at people I don't see anymore whom I don't want to see or whom I do want to see but I do nothing about it or whom I do see and wish I didn't. It seems that most often my screaming is about being betrayed, lied to, used, or manipulated. In the morning, all I want to do is be quiet. I don't want to think that the dreams might mean something. My anger doesn't bother me. But its meaning does. I worry my dreams will change my days. I wonder what I've stopped hiding that the dreams have come and come so strongly. I wonder if this is the real question and, if not, then what is?

Wind in the windows. Winter sun. When will it be spring? Is that it? When will it be spring?

It was early spring when I met Tom McGrath in Managua, the beginning of the rainy season. Tom wore black leather gloves. Was that a symptom of his sickness? He knew he was dying. We stayed up late one night, talking. I was drinking beer. I don't remember what Tom was drinking. In fact, I don't even remember exactly what we said, that drifting kind of conversation which is about the layering of one person's story over the other:

Riding a boxcar
When I was in Paris
There were all these children
All these flowers
So I met my wife
I wrote a book
It was so cold the night
It was morning

What I remember is the effect of the night. I remember a quiet force in the man that moved me. *I didn't even know at the time who he was.* But I remember wanting to find out. I looked for his poems and found out about his life as a poet, as a teacher and organizer whose—what? politics? beliefs?—had almost marginalized him. Because whoever it is that arbitrates these kinds of things wouldn't take Tom's poetry seriously because somehow Tom didn't seem to "properly" acknowledge poetry's primacy in his life. Writing poetry was something Tom did, he did it beautifully and movingly, wittily, playfully, but the doing was only a part of, not all of, his way of life. He'd been blacklisted during the McCarthy era and it wasn't until the end of Tom's life that he even began to receive a fraction of the acclaim—a Guggenheim Fellow, an NEA Senior Fellow, a Shelley Memorial Award—our great artists deserve.

Tom's focus has meant a lot to me. It reminds me, in those small moments when I feel marginalized (where is your book, where is your book, little voices scraping at my bones) because of larger work I want to do (politics on the sleeve, part of the teaching, part of the talking, part of why I breathe and eat). Because I am writing. I'm writing all the time. But the words, the words give way to other moments, other actions that are larger and more significant to me, literature as a function of life, and not the other way around. As in Alta. Her sisters. *Their world and mine.*

I know this vision is true. But doubt. Doubt. Tom is dead. He's been dead for years. I can't find Alta. I don't even know where to look. I saw Tom only that one time in Nicaragua. Ten years ago. My memories of Alta are fading. Tom's books aren't enough for me. They're all I have. And these dreams. Too much anger. Loss. The rolling together of my life in a way that's so hard to understand.

—*Mark Statman*

II. The Loss Poem as Memory and Memorial

There are a number of ways to begin talking about loss. For me the simplest is the most successful: I just ask the students if they've ever lost something. They talk about toys.

What was it?

A doll.

A baseball.

A book.

And how did that feel?

It made me sad. I couldn't find it and it was something I really liked.

It made me feel stupid. I was certain I knew exactly where it was. For a while I thought someone had stolen it.

Why were these things so important, I ask.

Shrugs.

Because we liked them?

You like your dinner, I say, but you don't miss it when it's gone.

Dinner is supposed to disappear. These kinds of things aren't.

But why are't they?

Because, someone ventures, they were things that were supposed to stay parts of our lives.

And when you lose them?

It's like a part of our lives is gone and we can't get it back.

Sometimes the students talk about how some losses, such as toys, aren't as important as others. They don't mind them as much. Occasionally someone brings up losing in games. They talk about how angry it makes them to lose.

Why?

Because losing isn't fun. We worked hard to win and we didn't. We don't like being beaten.

But doesn't someone have to lose in a game?

Sure, but that doesn't mean you have to like it.

We also talk about how some kinds of things are harder to lose than others. Someone *has* to be the loser in a game. But many of the students talk about how it doesn't feel right that more important things are lost too—a pet, a relative, a friend. They agree that it is natural, but they don't like it. The inevitability of loss can be bewildering.

Several times I've been in classrooms where one of the students has recently lost a relative. Everyone is aware of what has happened and you can feel the sadness in the room. Sometimes it's awkward: Do we talk about this? How? Often, it's the students themselves who open the conversation, to tell you what they need to say. I remember one first grader, whose mother had just died, jumping up as soon as I walked into the room to tell me what had happened. He insisted that we talk about it, so we did. We talked about what he was thinking and feeling. His classmates asked him questions.

Are you scared? Are you lonely?

Some talked about their own kinds of losses, feeling connected—though not in the same depth as with the loss of a mother—because an aunt died or a dog ran away. But they felt close enough that they could empathize and understand.

A poem I've found extremely useful for helping me talk with students about loss is César Vallejo's "A mi hermano Miguel" or "To My Brother Miguel":

A mi hermano Miguel
in memoriam

Hermano, hoy estoy en el poyo de la casa,
donde nos haces una falta sin fondo!
Me acuerdo que jugábamos esta hora, y que mamá
nos acariciaba: "Pero hijos . . ."

Ahora yo me escondo,
como antes, todas estas oraciones
vespertinas, y espero que tú no des conmigo.
Por la sala, el zaguán, los corredores.
Después, te ocultas tú, y yo no doy contigo.
Me acuerdo que nos hacíamos llorar,
hermano, en aquel juego.

Miguel, tú te escondiste
una noche de agosto, al alborear;
pero, en ves de ocultarte riendo, estabas triste.
Y tu gemelo corazón de esas tardes
extintas se ha aburrido de no encontrarte. Y ya
cae sombra en el alma.

Oye hermano, no tardes
en salir. Bueno? Puede inquietarse mamá.

   —*Cesar Vallejo*

To My Brother Miguel
in memoriam

Brother, today I sit on the stone bench of our house
where you make an emptiness without end
I remember how we used to play at this time, and that Mama
would caress us: "Now boys!"

And now I'm hiding myself
as before, from all those evening prayers
and I hope you don't find me.
In the living room, in the entrance, the corridors.
Later, you hide, and I don't find you.
I remember how it made us cry,
brother, this game.

Miguel, you hid yourself
one night in August at dawn
but instead of hiding laughing, you were sad
And your twin heart of those extinct
afternoons has grown tired of not finding you. And now
a shadow falls on the soul.

Look, brother, don't be late
leaving. Okay? You know Mama worries.

I like how quiet the poem is, how it moves through death and games, the mother's worry, the wistful hope of the brother's return. The images of the poem are striking: the caressing hands of the mother, of the house with its stone bench, the halls and rooms. I'm drawn, too, to the idea of dying as a sad kind of hiding. I'm always moved by Vallejo's idea of the shadow that falls on the soul.

When I teach "To My Brother Miguel," I ask my students to think about the poet's use of memory, how it exists as a kind of memorial and, as such, is a way of keeping his brother in his life. Although his brother doesn't live, Vallejo is able to have him around and keep part of his own youth with him as well. In a way, he's doing what some of the students I've worked with have suggested the uses of memory are: they re-create and thus maintain reality.

Teaching loss has come up in other ways. One, in particular, stands out for me. In the spring of 1996, I was working with a group of sixth graders. We had read Tom McGrath's poem "When We Say Goodbye," and as we began to talk about it I realized that, in a way, this poem was about us.

When We Say Goodbye

It is not because we are going—
Though the sea may begin at the doorstep, though the highway
May already have come to rest in our front rooms . . .

It is because, beyond distance, or enterprise
And beyond the lies and surprises of the wide and various worlds,
Beyond the flower and the bird and the little boy with his large
    questions . . .
We notice our shadows:
Going . . .
—slowly, but going,

In slightly different directions—
Their speeds increasing—
Growing shorter, shorter
As we enter the intolerable sunlight that never grows old or kind.

I'd been working with this particular group of students since they were in first grade. I'd known them for half their lives and yet, when this school year ended, it was more than likely I'd never see most of them again. When I mentioned this to them, it generated an extraordinary discussion about time, growing up, how it affects people and relationships. After that class, I noticed that our remaining days together seemed to take on a kind of urgency. The lines of our lives were moving further apart almost before our eyes. There seemed to be no idle time when I was there, no fooling around. It was almost as though we'd collectively and unconsciously decided that every second I was with them was too important and meaningful to waste.

Sometimes the experience of reading and then writing loss poems can make these poems heartbreaking as the students use it as a way to talk about themselves.

My father
was tough.
My father
was the one
I loved and
I was the
one he loved.
I also love
my mother
just like
she loves
me. And
if one of
them dies
I would
feel like
the sunrise
was falling off
the earth.
And one day
guess what
it happened

my father
died
and one day
my mother
was crying
I said oh no
oh no what
happpened Mom?
Your father died
Oh, no. And then
I cried
I felt
like
the sunrise
fell off
the earth
Oh no father

   —Romaine Thomas, third grade

In the daytime I hear
birds singing in the trees.
And I hear the train.
I see gray eyes.
I am sad.
I had cats.
I have lost all my cats.

   —Keya Walters, first grade

Sitting in the dark room
thinking and feeling that the room is
caving in on me, pain

sorrow, tears, feelings I feel
within my heart and soul, life is
bitter and all alone, what have I

done, I have hidden my
fears away in a lonesome world but
I have to regain them

because without fear you live
not, without hope you feel not, within

the angels shooting arrows around
love has faded away and sorrow has
found its way within you

 —*Brenda Ayala, sixth grade*

The White Horse

Up on the hill so
you almost touch the
sky. You feel so close
you want to touch them.
A gust of wind seems
to swipe my troubles
out of my mind. The
hill twisting around. Tall
grass up to your knees.
The carved horse of
rock crumbling away from
erosion. It falls away
till it's gone forever.
I turn around and see
factories, smoke, cars
slip into my head.

 —*Robert Hackett, fifth grade*

Eternal Instants

As water runs down a blade of grass
And time draws near like rising rain
We must set ourselves in motion
The bell has rung
It's time for the next class
But not a sound was heard
With the wind on our backs
And the sun in our faces
The trek towards the next hello
And away from the last good-bye
Is instantaneous yet eternal
For good-bye lasts an eternity
Yet hello is a moment lost forever
I see a light

As I bid
Farewell

   —*Joey Alexiou, sixth grade*

Good-bye

Good-bye to you
I will be back
I promise I will
I will not be gone as long as the universe exists or as
          long as the air is here
Remember
my living soul will always be with you when I'm gone
I will come back through the light
say hello
touch your hand

   —*Michael Schiralli, sixth grade*

III. About Writing about Loss

I wonder sometimes about the sadness of the poems I teach and of the sadness of the poems they generate. For one thing, sadness doesn't fit in with the regular curriculum. On one level, this apprehension may simply be that certain words, ideas, and images sometimes seem inappropriate for a particular place. But on a more complex level, I wonder how far as a teaching poet I can (or ought to) go with the younger students. When I ask them to open up, they will often write in the personal, private, and revelatory way that poetry allows. This is a good thing, and when it happens there's an obvious growth in the critical and creative consciousness of the students, a greater sense of understanding about who they are. Still, this is tricky territory, and I know that as the facilitator of this process it's my responsibility, along with the teachers with whom I work, to make sure that the students feel as safe as possible about writing creatively, intelligently, and honestly about themselves. If neither the teacher nor I believe that this sense of safety exists, then this kind of lesson is one I will not do.

Some teachers I've worked with have talked about how important and powerful they think it is that students, in writing their poetry, have the opportunity for "getting it out." Too often, though, I've found that what teachers mean by "getting it out" is getting rid of it, allowing the students to say what's on their minds and then forgetting it.

However, writing about sadness is not about forgetting. It's more about naming sadness, describing it, and trying to figure out how to accept or not accept it. The truth is, if the poem is a successful one, it means every time they read it they'll actually, actively relive their sadness.

Writing as therapy is tricky territory, and I think it's important here to make a distinction between writing as therapy and writing as art. As therapy, writing is placed in a context in which the therapist tries to help the writer figure out what the written work means to the writer. The *only* focus is on the specific *usefulness* of the writing. In art, however, the writer exercises craft, control. He or she is moving through content, probably and potentially as a way of understanding something new in his or her life, but also more *formally* as a way of figuring out the best way to say something. It's not just the idea of the work, it's the presentation. The largeness of craft, with its stress on the writer's voice, the writer's style, the writer's authority over form and content means that the created piece takes on its own importance independent of the writer. We don't need to know who wrote a poem or a story to appreciate it or enjoy it, become inspired or reflective.

Writing imaginatively and personally about loss has the potential for blurring the lines beween writing as therapy and writing as art. When I'm considering teaching loss poems, I'll speak with teachers ahead of time to find out how appropriate they feel it would be for their students. Usually, and especially in cases where there have been difficult losses, the teachers with whom I've worked have wanted the students to read poems like Vallejo's and McGrath's, and to have their students write on the subject and then read their work to each other. Doing so allows students to talk about things that are not usually discussed in school. Personal loss is not something that immediately opens itself up to group or classroom discussion. Yet school can be a place where these discussions work well because good classrooms provide a fundamental requirement: trust on the part of the participants that they'll be listened to and responded to, and faith that that trust won't be abused.* Creating this environment in a classroom has a lot more to do with the teachers and the students than it

---

* These classrooms usually have a number of distinguishing characteristics; they are ones in which, through the collaborative efforts of the teachers and students, there are regular class meetings, the agenda of which is not dominated by the teacher but is open to everyone in the class. These classrooms also usually have access to due process and peer mediation.

does with the presence of the once-a-week visiting poet. What I can do, though, is be someone who can be trusted. For me, this isn't hard. I love reading and writing poetry. I love teaching and I take my teaching seriously. Being in a classroom and doing something that's so important makes it easy for me to take seriously the ideas, feelings, and opinions of everyone in the class.

When asking students to write personally, I am careful to make sure they don't feel pressured to reveal things they don't want other people to know. And when they do write about things that are deeply personal, I make sure they don't feel pressured into talking about them. I remember one of my college students talking once about how when she was in elementary school, a relative of hers had died and she'd had to miss school. When she returned to school, her teacher—to my student's horror—announced the death to the class. My student was devastated, feeling as though an important part of her private life, her grief, was now public property.

When I ask students to write about *anything*, I generally do not force them to read their work out loud. One time a student had written a moving elegy for a relative who had died of AIDS. He was stunned by the death, he told me, and happy to have had the chance to write about it. When I asked him if he wanted to read it to his classmates, he shook his head and started to cry. It was too private, he said. He didn't want to read it and he didn't want to publish it in our anthology. He felt it was enough for him to have written it.

Later, I remember talking with his teacher about this. She remarked on how happy she was to know that her classroom had been safe enough for the student to write the poem, that he understood that no matter what he wrote, his privacy would be respected.

Chapter 6

Going Places, Seeing Places: On Descriptive Writing

I. Place and Perspective: Changing Points of View

is there a poem in fishing?

> *Nimrod fishing: pike, smallmouth bass,*
> *sunfish, redeye, trout*

is there a poem in fishing?
as in writing the river
as in the cold there and
the size of the sky
and the trees hanging over
then this:
the surprise that
a redeye's eyes really are a bright flooded red
when a bass takes the hook
it pauses
pauses
you can feel it then, soft, quick
on the line
it pulls and pulls
pike have tiny teeth, sharp, avoid
the yellow in the sunfish
is the yellow in the sun
the brilliant morning one
that burns the early fog
off the day
a rainbow trout's rainbow
sits in your wet hand
the fish struggles, its life, slapping
until you remove the hook
problem of the barb
and set the rainbow back in the water
the way you've done it before

every fish from the river
back to the river
where the fish live
where the poem starts

—*Mark Statman*

Where we are affects how we think. When I'm riding my mountain bike hard through the woods, my thinking is usually about where I am, what I'm seeing, and how I respond to the beauty aesthetically (the gorgeousness of nature) and physically (adjusting my speed to the difficulty of the trail). If I'm at the beach on a warm summer day, the water and sand and people make me feel more relaxed. I don't think about teaching. I don't think about paying bills. If the beach were empty or if the sun were setting, my thinking might become more inward (memories of other days at the beach, ideas for a poem or a story). On the other hand, on the subway, I tend to avoid looking at what's around me. I read a book or magazine. I confess that I might even use the subway time to grade papers.

Places can affect not only our thinking of the moment, but also the ways in which we subsequently think about our lives. The first time I saw the Luxemburg Gardens in Paris, I was twenty-four years old, on my honeymoon, and I started to cry. I couldn't believe how beautiful it was, a sunny day in early fall, early fall flowers, early fall trees, green, orange, gold. I couldn't believe that I'd been alive twenty-four years and never seen this. It seemed a shame to have lived that long and not known this beauty. And it seemed amazing, too, how ready I was at that moment— the happiness of my marriage, the strangeness of this new to me but old city, its architecture and gardens, the people—and ready in a way I never could have been before that moment. Had I seen it earlier, I'd never have been able to respond as completely as I was responding just then. I also remember the sadness of thinking that, as many times as I might again be able to see this, I'd never again have the experience of seeing it for the first time.

When teaching poems about place, I often begin by asking my students to think about places they've been that have surprised or moved them, to think about places they've been that have made them feel comfortable or happy, that they may or may not know well, and to which they might like to return. We talk about how this can be a place that is far-away and exotic, or it can be some place that seems ordinary to others (a bedroom, a backyard) but meaningful to the writer. As they begin to remember or imagine these places, I ask them to try to picture those places in their head, to think about how they might describe those places and to think about how they might describe the effect those places have on them. After we've talked about these places, I show them Gary Snyder's "Work to Do toward Town."

Work to Do toward Town

Venus glows in the east,
  mars hangs in the twins.
Frost on the logs and bare ground
  free of house or tree.
Kites come down from the mountains
And glide quavering over the rooftops;
  frost melts in the sun.
A low haze hangs on the houses
  —firewood smoke and mist—
Slanting far to the Kamo river
  and the distant Uji hills.
Farmwomen lead down carts
  loaded with long white radish;
I pack my bike with books—
  all roads descend toward town.

In Snyder's poem, every line points the reader's eye in a different direction, almost as though we readers are moving our heads to see what's going on. Snyder's descriptions are so specific and concrete you can actually draw the poem (which I do on the blackboard, showing the rising sun, the hovering birds, the haze, the farmwomen, the poet with his bicycle). "Work to Do toward Town" is like a brief cinematic pan of the valley. No matter how long it took Snyder to write the poem, what's happening in the poem takes only a short amount of time to occur and an equally short amount of time to see. This poem cannot be about a lengthy moment because soon Venus, the morning star, will no longer be visible (the sun will be too bright). With the arrival of the sun, the frost will melt. The kites will hover for only so long over the village before they fly away. The women must get their crops to the market in town (and then have enough time to do their own buying and get back home).

After presenting this photographically descriptive poem, I go back to our discussion of the places the students have previously remembered and ask them to think about how they might describe these places. I remind them that it's exciting to make the place vivid for the reader, to make the poem as descriptive as possible. Before they begin I ask them to try to be specific about time and, as they get a clear picture in their heads, to try to round out that picture by including the other senses. What can they smell, hear, taste, or feel? I remind them of how much action there is in Snyder's poem, that despite how quiet his early morning poem is, its action is what makes the moment. How much activity might there be in the small moment they're describing? How will, or won't, the place in their poems change as the moment they're describing passes?

Sunrise NYC

the sun is rising
above the water
at the beach
sea gulls fly over the water
for food
the wind blowing
on the water
but the sky is blue
with water color
up here the sand castles
wash away

—*Aleson Espinosa, fifth grade*

the desert

while the snake moves
the sun boils
and while the beetles roam
the blue sky moves
like a cloud

—*Brian LeBouef, fourth grade*

Sunset

Look up into the sky
gleaming sun blinding me
golden like blooming sunflowers
like fire burning
shining like a brand-new pair of
shoes
it's a wonderful sight

turn my head
look back
it's gone
burning fire
sunflowers
shine
    gone
        sunset

  —Stephanie German, fifth grade

I went in my mind
I went to Maine
It was beautiful
I saw flowers and green grass
There were streets and people
The people were saying *hot dogs*
This was scary
I flew to a place that was cold

I was at the South Pole
I saw snow
There were mountains and rocks
falling down the
mountains
I drank hot coffee
There was a
big loud sound
I was going to my house
I was a little scared
I woke up
I saw myself in bed
I said, This is a quiet place
the place I want

  —Mariana Vidal, fourth grade

Tennessee

Slingshots shoot rocks
rocks of dust
oil cans next to
orange cars
different colored birds
forests no leaves
dusty old

tractor red
garden dead
houses with
people living on a farm
founder of a farm
farm community

   —Fahd Malik, fourth grade

The Pond

The pond wants to take me away
Away from the tender spot where I lay
A swan and duck pass by
letting out a stirring cry
But all I do is let out a sigh

The roots make several steps
As though they want me to climb
But I can do nothing with these lazy feet
of mine

   —Becky Kish, fourth grade

*   *   *

Pablo Neruda's "The Sea" offers students a different perspective on description of place. Neruda does not attempt an objective description of the ocean. Rather, he describes the ocean ecstatically, a "university of waves," where he finds himself transformed. Neruda, whose native Chile has a border that is almost half shoreline, is not alien to the place of the poem—he is completely and determinedly a part of it. The describing here is not of the foreign, but of the familiar.

El Mar

Necesito del mar porque me enseña:
no sé si aprendo música o conciencia:
no sé si es ola sola o ser profundo
o sólo ronca voz o deslumbrante
suposición de peces y navíos.
El hecho es que hasta cuando estoy dormido
de algún modo magnético circulo
en la universidad de oleaje.

No son sólo las conchas trituradas
como si algún planeta tembloroso
participara paulatina muertes,
no, del fragmento reconstryo el día,
de una racha de sal la estalactita
y de una cucharada el dios inmenso.

Lo que antes me enseñó lo guardo! Es aire,
incesante viento, agua y arena.

Parece poco para el hombre joven
que aqui llegó a vivir con sus incendios,
y sin embargo el pulso que subia
y bajaba a su abismo,
el frío del azul que crepitaba,
el desmoronamiento de la estrella,
el tierno desplegarse de la ola
despilfarrando nieve con la espuma,
el poder quíeto, allí, determinado
como un trono de piedra en lo profundo,
sustituyó el recinto en que crecián
tristeza terca, amontonando, olvido,
y cambió bruscamente mi existencia:
di mi adhesión el puro movimiento.

   —Pablo Neruda

The Sea

I need the ocean because it teaches me;
I don't know if it's music or myself that I learn,
I don't know if it's from a single wave or something deeper,
from the ocean's roaring voice or its brilliant
collection of fishes and boats.
The fact is, even when I'm asleep,
by some magnetic circle's trick,
I'm in the university of waves.

It's not only the conch shells shattered
by the trembling
of a planet slowly dying,
because from looking at one shell fragment
I can remake the day,
from a grain of salt, I can make a tower,
and with a spoonful of ocean, God.

Everything it teaches me, I keep. It is air,
endless wind, water and sand.

It doesn't seem like much to the young people
who come here to live with their fires,
but the water pulse goes up
and down in the deep,
the blue cold freezes,
the stars' reflection glitters
the endless tide with its waves
throwing snow with the foam,
its quiet power, is all there, determined,
like a stone you throw into the deep;
all this takes away the sadness
that can grow in me, the growing oblivion,
it suddenly changes my whole life:
held so tightly to the pure movement.

At first, "The Sea" is tough for the kids. There's a lot going on in the poem—what Neruda learns, the somewhat metaphysical ideas that the ocean makes him wonder about, the sources of those wonderings—but the students eventually get it. A key here is to have them think hard and talk about what they know about the sea and what it makes them wonder about, before we look at Neruda's poem. That way, they're prepared for the similarities and the differences between themselves and Neruda. This discussion involves a lot of brainstorming. I write all their ideas on the blackboard. They tell me about sea creatures, geological formations, colors, the uses of the ocean, its environmental significance (food, oxygen, pollution), its economy (fishing, transportation, fuel), scientific research, and about why it's fun to go to the ocean (swimming, surfing, looking at it makes you wonder). We also talk about how dangerous the ocean can be (sharks, shipwrecks, tidal waves, and powerful riptides).

Then, when we look at Neruda's poem, the children are drawn to the power the ocean has for him, his description of it as "the university of waves." His idea of the power of his own imagination—how he can remake the day, make a tower, even see God—fascinates the students. These few lines have generated some wonderful discussions about the students' own imaginations, because they too have been able to do what Neruda does: have visions and construct worlds.

Oddly enough, the students often agree with the line "It doesn't seem like much to the young people." They talk about how children think of the beach as just a place to play, rather than as a place to think or wonder. I ask them, though, if they think that Neruda meant them, the young people in the room, when he wrote the line. Though they don't seem to experience as deeply as Neruda does the ocean's transformative powers, they realize they are not the young people of his poem because they've already demonstrated how much the ocean means to them.

The Ocean

As I stand with
my feet in the sand
and the wind blowing through
my hair, I see and hear
the waves splashing and the
sounds of the birds above
and the moon shining down
on the waves. I hear a
steady drumbeat. Then all
the birds go to sleep
and all you can hear
is the waves making a
drumbeat.

    —Sarah Lynch, fifth grade

The Ocean

I see . . . little waves
and big waves and smell the
salty air

I dive into the water and see the hot,
yellow, shiny sand
right on the ground
that blows into the water and keeps
getting smaller and smaller and
smaller

    —Sherri Chester, fifth grade

Horses of the Sea

Sitting on the shore
waves move in
the horses of the sea
start rolling in
loud big horses

come in and out
horses of the sea rolling about

Horses of the sea push the boat
and the whales
that go
for a float
horses run on land in
big large noisy bands

   —*Jeffrey Spencer, fifth grade*

A Pleasant Morning

A single ray of sunshine hits my
face

The furious palms crash before
swaying palm trees

A tired man lies peacefully in
a hammock

While sea gulls sing a squawking
song over the green, blue ocean

And my toes tingle in
the sparkling white
sand

   —*Nicolas DiPietro, fifth grade*

Missing

I look at the beach
and see just a plain old
blue beach.
I look out the second
time and prove myself
wrong.
There is something I have
missed.
I wonder, what could I
have missed. Maybe its
mystical way of showing
itself.
I wonder what is on the

other side and if people
see me, hear me, feel
me.
I walk out and step
into the salty water.
The seashells crunch under
my feet.
Its warmth and comfort
is a strength.
The waves swish over
my feet sending a
loving message to my
brain. All is quiet, still,
motionless. I know now
the beauty of life.
I see what I have
missed.

—*Alison Post, fifth grade*

The Ocean

I hear the whales sing
The waves slap my feet
I step on many shells
The water is cold and slippery
There is a wake that pushes my feet
My feet get tangled in bunches of seaweed
I go on shore and watch dolphins
I go back in the water
and then again I feel the
sugar ground and rocks and shells
at my feet
I pick up coral and
I put it in a bucket
I feel creature movements
I see whales shoot water out of their blowholes
The dolphins jump out of the water
I swim all around
The cold water goes through my hair
I swim with the dolphins
I go to shore, baby crabs nibble at my feet
I laugh

All of a sudden, everything stops
I stop, this poem stops
   —Dina Melamed, fifth grade

II. Wherever I Hang My Hat Isn't Home: Writing Poems about Travel

A Mexican Clock
(*excerpt*)

you spend too much time
color yellow to color red color heart
you spend a minute and the light
goes too crazy on your eyes
the black green mountains begin to move with your heartbeat
a bump bump jump sway
you spend an hour and the darkness
the shadow of half-seeing
or half-seen
strange boys and girls looking
as hard at you as you do at them
unearthly your paleness
unearthly their silence
(it trails off in the night
quietness of appearance and disappearance
of underneath, of the moon, of the earth)
exhausted
you draw a map of the city in the sand
and then a man comes along
he's a thousand years old
a straw hat white guayabera white pantalones huaraches
and he brushes your map away and says
look for it in your eyes

what eyes
unable to see in all the usual ways
darkness framing the squareness of houses
lavender lime and yellow under lights
darkness framing the squares of faces
and plazas
trees gardens gates
cornering the angles into life
the sounds from a radio
quién como tú

the one two three
of a burro and a man walking down
the stone street
amplified insect buzz
of insects, cars and trucks
going in and out away . . .

—*Mark Statman*

In going other places, I've learned how to be at home. Travelling reminds me how important it is not to take the things and people of my everyday life for granted. When I travel, I expect new experiences, to be surprised. Even when I'm visiting places I know well, I look to see what's changed and what's remained the same. It is easy not to do this when I'm at home, oblivious to the world outside. When we see things every day, it's easy to ignore them and forget how valuable they are. It's also easy to forget about the rest of the world and that what seems so vital and significant in one place may have no importance someplace else. New York City may be the center of the world to people living there, but to those in San Francisco, in Luxemburg, in Rio de Janeiro? I remember once I was driving through the rain-forest mountains in the state of Oaxaca in Mexico. The air was thick with mist and the jungle seemed so dark, green, mysterious, and exciting. At a tiny restaurant, I started talking with the teenaged girl who was serving me. She asked me where I was from.

The United States.

I've heard of it, she said.

New York City.

This drew a blank. She'd never heard of New York. She'd heard of the city of Oaxaca, yes, but had never been there. In fact, she added, she'd never been out of the mountains.

I found this unbelievable. But then I wondered why I should. Why should I expect that she'd know what I knew? Why did I think that she'd want to live the way that I did? My immediate assumption had been that she lived as she did not by choice but because she had neither the education nor the money to live any "better." But our conversation suggested that she felt no need to be anywhere other than where she was. Later, I wondered if maybe she thought I was a little sad. What was I doing so far from home? Wasn't I happy there?

I've often told this story as an introduction to teaching Elizabeth Bishop's "Questions of Travel." It's a long poem that I've used at the college level, but I've found that most fifth and sixth graders with whom I've worked for extended periods have enjoyed it a great deal. In particular, they become caught up in Bishop's language, which is extraordinarily lush and rich (like the setting in the poem) but whose fast, breathless lines propel the poem along swiftly (like the waterfall-to-be of her poem). They are also intrigued by Bishop's dilemma: which is better, to travel in the imagination and avoid being a gawking tourist or to have the eye-opening and potentially breathtaking experiences that travel gives us? They also like to think about what it means to be a tourist. Some find the idea of themselves as the objects of tourism—that someone from someplace else might come and observe them—oddly disturbing. One sixth grader once remarked that it was almost as though people were looking at one other the way people look at animals in the zoo. One girl turned to him and said, "That's scary and weird but it's also true."

Questions of Travel

There are too many waterfalls here; the crowded streams
hurry too rapidly down to the sea,
and the pressure of so many clouds on the mountaintops
makes them spill over the sides in soft slow-motion,
turning to waterfalls under our very eyes.
—For if those streaks, those mile-long, shiny tearstains,
aren't waterfalls yet,
in a quick age or so, as ages go here,
they probably will be.
But if the streams and clouds keep travelling, travelling,
the mountains look like the hulls of capsized ships,
slime-hung and barnacled.

Think of the long trip home.
Should we have stayed at home and thought of here?
Where should we be today?
Is it right to be watching strangers in a play
in this strangest of theatres?
What childishness is it that while there's a breath of life
in our bodies, we are determined to rush
to see the sun the other way around?
The tiniest green hummingbird in the world?
To stare at some inexplicable old stonework,
inexplicable and impenetrable,

at any view,
instantly seen and always, always delightful?
Oh, must we dream our dreams
and have them too?
And have we room
for one more folded sunset, still quite warm?

But sure it would have been a pity
not to have seen the trees along this road
really exaggerated in their beauty,
not to have seen them gesturing
like noble pantomimists, robed in pink.
—Not to have had to stop for gas and heard
the sad, two-noted, wooden tune
of disparate wooden clogs
carelessly clacking over
a grease-stained filling-station floor.
(In another country the clogs would all be tested.
Each pair there would have identical pitch.)
—A pity not to have heard
the other, less primitive music of the fat brown bird
who sings above the broken gasoline pump
in a bamboo church of Jesuit baroque:
three towers, five silver crosses.
—Yes, a pity to have pondered,
blurr'dly and inconclusively,
on what connection can exist for centuries
between the crudest footwear
and, careful and finicky,
the whittled fantasies of wooden cages.
—Never to have studied history in
the weak calligraphy of songbirds' cages.
—And never to have had to listen to rain
so much like politicians' speeches:
two hours of unrelenting oratory
and then a sudden golden silence
in which the traveller takes a notebook, writes:

*"Is it a lack of imagination that makes us come
to imagined places, not to just stay at home?
Or could Pascal have been not entirely right
about just sitting quietly in one's room?*

*Continent, city, country, society:
the choice is never wide and never free.*

And here, or there . . . No. Should have we stayed at home,
wherever that may be?"

When teaching "Questions of Travel," I ask the students to think about how they think Bishop might have been influenced by where she was. We look at how colorfully she describes a colorful place, how the words of the poem somehow sound like the place, as in "the careless clacking of clogs" and "the unrelenting oratory" of politicians. I point out other ways in which the poem relies on sound, the golden silence, for example, at the ending of the rain. I ask them to compare the end of the poem to the rest of it, pointing out how vague the description of home is, "wherever that may be." Evan, a fifth grader, said he'd noticed this: "It's because she's not paying attention to what's around her, she's paying attention to what's in her head."

In getting students started on their writing, I ask them to think about places to which they've traveled. I tell them they can wonder about their own questions about travel, and that they might also think of their own reasons for traveling. Some may go for fun or because it's their parents' idea, but some of the students write about travel in a way that comes close to my own sense of its value: yes, it is about having a good time, but it's also about learning.

Epcot at Night

I'm waiting around the dock at Epcot
soon it gets dark
the lights on the Eiffel Tower shut down
Germany
Norway
China
everything goes dark
I can see over the water the boats leaving
and the ducks going to sleep
the sun is now setting it's beautiful
I can still remember it
Boom!
The first firework goes off
I can see it in the sky
It's purple and it leaves a shadow
each one goes off one by one

Boom!
Boom!

    —Alina Bova, fifth grade

A Place in Imagination

Imagining a place
In my room
A place of forests
Thinking should I go

Yes, I think
But what if
I go and
It is not
What I imagined
And I am left alone disappointed with
only memories
of my own
imagination

But if I go
and
It's better than
what I have imagined
Wow!

Yes
If I go then I can
still have my fantasy
and save it for another
place

But what if it's
the same
I am left
alone disappointed
with only memories

So . . .
Should I stay in my room
my home
Or leave and be free?

    —Kristyn Forte, sixth grade

At Peace

When I look at peace
I see nothing
What is peace
Is peace a tree?
Is a tree at peace?
Thinking of nothing
Doing nothing,
Shedding its leaves like the burdens of the world.
When you finally find
Your own personal peace
Like the end of a war
Or pure simplicity
Does it cause other things
To suffer because
You've found your peace?
Maybe they
Are upset because
Their vision of peace is different
From yours
Or mine
Is my vision of peace right or wrong,
Or is it
Both?

    —Ben Jackson, sixth grade

I Don't Know Me

It was a Massachusetts day,
a beautiful hot summer day
Grass with bright green color
sky a beautiful
blue with swirls of
white
White churches
gardens of pink and
yellow and red tulips
blue and white
roses, picket fences
open shops
sprinklers, music
parades walking down
the dirt road
and the way to enjoy it

is with a picnic
just how my family and I are
enjoying it . . .
But I can't enjoy
the flowers and parades
and church bells
as we sit on the
picnic blanket pulling
out our lunch
I feel low and dark
I want to break free
I want to know the cure
I have a feeling
of a lonely woman
I hear the parade
I feel the cool but
hot wind surrounds me
I feel the happiness
but I can't see
the lady anymore
She's in my mind
I would think
but I know everything
about myself
Is there more that I have
to know about myself?
So I can meet myself
I can see myself
I can meet the
lonely woman inside me

   —Chloe Seitz, sixth grade

Chapter 7

Listener in the Snow: Writing Poems about the Seasons

Hold On

Summer always ends too soon. It ends before it starts. It ends before you think about it. It ends just as you say this is what I'm going to do. And the leaves are red and yellow, bright, leaving the trees. There's snow on the ground. It covers the entire city. You can't hear anything and all you can see is white and ice.

Different memories skate by. When I was small, there were all these snowdrifts and school closed. Cold snow goes down my neck and it gets red there. The snow of snowball-making sticks in the wool of my gloves and won't come out no matter how hard I clap. Sometimes my mother makes hot chocolate. Sometimes I shovel the walk and I don't want to. None of us tries to be efficient about it. And it doesn't get any easier that way. It gets harder. The way as you get older you accumulate more things: papers, books, furniture, relationships, until suddenly you can't put them anywhere and even when you move to a bigger house, you still can't get a bigger life. Like old letters and leftover money from other countries, you can't throw life away. Words connect to things. Green plastic glass with water equals green plastic glass with water. Green oak leaf equals green oak leaf. But love? It equals the growing wilderness of the past, present, and future like white sea birds that hover between the ocean, the sky, and the ground. It equals the horizon way far out there. It equals trees. Or streets. Or a market where everything in the world is for sale. The market spills into the streets, people touching and bargaining, fruit, vegetables, and flowers, mysterious, compelling pieces of machinery, clothing, rugs.

Spring sneaks in because there's still snow on the ground. It brings cold to warm wind and cold to warm rain. It's easier to move because you want to be outside. All the rooms have grown so small and we've been stumbling through them for months, dizzy, blind moths bumping into walls. We have these cages we've built that we don't want to have anymore. Or at least not now. You can hear radios and voices of people talking, surprised in their walks. They say, how *are* you, I haven't seen you in so long.

Then it's over. Suddenly. A humid shadow passes over like an uncertain angel. How many cycles are there? Never enough. I want one more than that. At least one more. At least as many so there's summer.

—*Mark Statman*

I like talking with kids about the seasons. I like their excitement about them, how vividly they can describe them and say what the seasons mean to them. It's hard to find someone who likes all of them completely, but it's also hard to find someone who really dislikes any of them. Even the ones who detest the cold of winter still like the way snow looks when it falls, or how they can play in it or celebrate the winter holidays. The ones who hate summer because it's too hot and there's nothing to do still like the fact that there's no school and they're "free." When I ask the students to write about the seasons, the struggle is to get them to go beyond the obvious.

Looking at Mario Benedetti's "Summer" (below) helps do this. Before we read the poem, I ask the students to think about their memories and experiences of the seasons. At first, the discussion generates a list of what they can do or have done. Some have gone to the beach or pool, others have gone skiing or ice skating. But then I ask the students to think more specifically about particular moments: what distinguished one afternoon of skiing from another, what can they visualize about a particular summer morning? I ask them to describe specifically the physical and emotional details of the moment: where did you feel the wind or the cold, where did you feel the sun or the water, what did that make you think of, what did that make you remember?

We then look at "Summer." The season calls and makes Benedetti not want to be where he is.

Verano

Voy a cerrar la tarde
se acabó
no trabajo
tiene la culpa el cielo
que urge como un río
tiene la culpa el aire
que está ansioso y no cambia
se acabó
no trabajo
tengo los dedos blandos

la cabeza remota
tengo los ojos llenos
de sueños
yo que sé
veo sólo paredes
se acabó
no trabajo
paredes con reproches
con órdenes
con rabia
pobrecitas paredes
con un solo almanaque
se acabó
no trabajo
que gira lentamente
dieciséis de diciembre

Iba a cerrar la tarde
pero suena el teléfono
si señor enseguida
comonó cuandoquiera

—*Mario Benedetti*

Summer

I'll close this afternoon
it's over
I can't work
the sky is to blame
it calls like a river
the air is to blame
it's anxious and unchanging
it's over
I can't work
I have soft hands
my head is gone
I have eyes full
of dreams
who knows
I see only walls
it's over
I can't work
walls that reproach me
with orders

with anger
poor little walls
with but a single calendar
it's over
I can't work
how slowly turns
this 16th of December

I was going to close early this afternoon
but the telephone rings
yes sir right away
ofcourse whendoyouwantit

When students read the poem, they're able to relate it instantly to the idea of how the season can affect you, how it makes you want to be someplace else or do something else. They like the humor of the poem, the angry walls, the closing lines, how someone (his boss? an important customer?) is thwarting his plans to get out of work. The repetition of "it's over / I can't work" also gives the poem a nice rhythm that many students imitate when they write their own seasons poems. The kids are always mystified that this poem, which takes place in December, is called "Summer." But Benedetti is from Uruguay, where the seasons are reversed. This sometimes makes for an interesting conversation—what's the difference between Christmas in South America and Christmas in New York? Would snow, Christmas trees, a red-suited Santa Claus and his sled make as much sense as symbols of Christmas in South America as they do in most parts of the United States? And what about places where there are only two seasons (rainy and dry)? What's the difference between life at the North Pole and life at the equator? What would life be like without any seasons at all? What would it be like with twice as many?

"Summer" provides a good model for asking the kids to find words and descriptions that they associate with the feelings and meanings of the season and to find ways to make them specific to that season, as Benedetti does with the languid anxiousness of an office worker in summer. Before they write, I remind them to think about our previous discussion about specific moments in the season. I ask the students to go beyond descriptions of a season and to include the effect the moment had on them: what does heat or rain or snow make them think about, make them want or not want? If the season or some part of it could speak to them, what might it say? Why does one season mean one thing while another means something else?

> It's sunny
> The sun is singing
> The butterfly is flying
> The girl pulled the flowers
> and it's raining
>
> —*Victor Garcia, kindergarten*

> It is snowing and
> snow is white
> paper can tear but snow
> can't tear
> I play and I make snowballs
> and snowmen and
> snow melts because it's ice water
> snow is good
> snow on a cold mountain
>
> —*Tatria Gooden, third grade*

Summer
Summer is the bright
sun that shines in the morning
and in the night it is dark
The moon shines
on the pictures that I draw
I see people smiling and
the sun said to me
float and come so we
could have fun
in the world
so we could go to space
and go under the water
and never go up
and see fish
blue gray orange and a blowfish
We are at the beach
but we must go home
and sleep
I will see you

next time
and now it is Fall

—*Jimmy Solano, second grade*

Fall

Fall is the season that the
leaves sing in the wind. They turn the
ground
     a   shimmering

golden brown and yellow and red. You hear
them talk when you crunch on them. The

     rushing wind
        whispers

in my ear. I feel happy. Happy is the
sky and ground

     and

          wind

—*Stephanie Bragman, fourth grade*

Weather

I wonder sometimes how do
the clouds in the sky show
so many beautiful colors
Whenever the sun shines
the sky is very blue
or when it does not shine
or when it is a rainy day
it is gray

Sometimes I like to go in the cool breeze
and listen to the birds chirp, the crickets
squealing and the squirrels moving
I like to go out into nature
and see the new world
I want to taste summer and see the beautiful
summer colors of leaves

Sometimes in the winter
it feels like I am on a mountain

having the time of my life,
skating on ice, smelling fresh
water, it could almost feel like
spring, little drops of ice
falling out of the sky
onto the ground, you
can feel the fresh drop of
water on your hands

In the fall, the leaves fall, and they have turned
beautiful colors
It seems they are dying to
the ground
The animals get ready for winter

Sometimes in the spring, the
birds come back from their homes
they soar through the air like airplanes
The squirrels come back too
They run very fast like someone is
chasing them
The bees and butterflies come back home

> —*Junior Griffiths, fifth grade*

In "Summer," Benedetti writes about the external effect of the season on the individual. In Wallace Stevens's "The Snow Man," the perspective is the opposite: to understand the winter, we must internalize it, become a part of it, see it as ourselves, as if we had become figures of snow.

The Snow Man

One must have a mind of winter
To regard the frost and the boughs
Of the pine-trees crusted with snow;

And have been cold a long time
To behold the junipers shagged with ice,
The spruces rough in the distant glitter

Of the January sun; and not to think
Of any misery in the sound of the wind,
In the sound of a few leaves,

Which is the sound of the land
Full of the same wind
That is blowing in the same bare place

For the listener, who listens in the snow,
And, nothing himself, beholds
Nothing that is not there and the nothing that is.

—*Wallace Stevens*

Like me, the students are intrigued by the idea of "a mind of winter":
just what is that? We think of other different kinds of minds you can have:
a mind of summer, a mind of ocean, a mind of wind, a mind of rock, a
mind of time. Looking at Stevens's poem, we talk about how that mind
considers ("regards") the world in a different way: cold is normal, ice and
glitter normal, there is no misery in all this as there might be for a human,
because it's what is to be expected and even desired. We talk about the
nothing of the poem, how the snow man who, in being nothing, can
behold only the nothing before him. I ask them to think about that noth-
ingness: what does it mean to them to think about nothing not as an
absence, but as a presence? I ask my students to pay attention, too, to
Stevens's language. It is often simple and clear, but Stevens also has a love
for the unexpected word or phrase ("junipers shagged," "spruces rough").
There's a nice formal tension between the poem's length (one sentence, if
thought of as prose) and the form of the three-line verses.

"The Snow Man" has inspired student writing that goes beyond the
descriptive poems that Benedetti's "Summer" yields. The idea of inter-
nalizing the moment of a particular season, of being one with it, has generated some surprising poems. While some of the students followed
Stevens's first line ("one must have a mind of pool to learn how to swim,"
"one must have a mind of rose in order to understand the flower"), the
students below seemed to go in more complex and exciting directions.
They wrote poems in which they defined the season, defined the situations, and defined the meaning. The seasons and situations of their poems
resemble ones we know, but there is something odd and new in them as
well.

Dark clouds mean rain
pink skies mean snow
when the moon is red
like a rose
think of red as hot days
as the days get longer

tell yourself summer
is near
as days and nights grow short
think of winter
as days seem normal
think of spring
as wind whistles and leaves fly
think of fall
to think of fall
think of trees growing bald
think of jumping in leaves
in summer
when the moon is red
like a red rose in the day
think of an Egyptian myth
stay with the present
and take weather as it is

    —*Effie Hirschfield, fifth grade*

The Nature Poets

Nature has snow and time
mixed together
On top of the grass
there is snow all the time
and insect wings are red
In space
there is snow
and the moon sets on the earth

    —*Michael Kovacik, first grade*

Impossible

When I went to sleep
I dreamed of
snow in the
summer and
it is wearing blue hands. He
got bigger and
changed into weird colors
and then he got
bigger
bigger
bigger

and bigger
and had muscles
that were bigger than
me and when
I woke up there
was snow in
the house

   —*Joseph Arcuri, third grade*

Los árboles

Los árboles crecen en la tierra
y crecen cuando nosotros crecemos
Los árboles crecen en la primavera
y en el verano
Cuando es otoño se caen las hojas
porque casi viene el invierno
Las hojas se cambian asi
primero verde
rojo armarillo
anaranjado café
despues se caen todo
menos uno

The Trees

The trees grow in the ground
and they grow when we grow
The trees grow in the spring
and summer
When it's fall, the leaves fall
because winter has almost come
The leaves change like this
first green
then yellow
then orange brown
then they all fall
except one

   —*Lydia Bernardez, third grade*

These Days

I'm sleeping well
I can never remember my dreams

I love how the sunshine
comes through the shades
and wakes me just in time for school
It feels like I'm still asleep
but then I go to the sink and
splash water on my face
POOF I'm awake
I rise and shine
faster than the morning
sun

   —Joe Guccione, fifth grade

Chapter 8

Sleeping and Dreaming

I. My Insomnia and El Coco de la Noche: Writing about Dreams

La avenida de sueños rotos

hearts
fall by
the sidewalks
hard
like this sun
falling into the west
of an ocean
quietly
you watch
and want to say something
smart like
no
it isn't better this way
the hand waving
like a magician's wand
this was a false one
walking as fast as it could
offstage
to let you know
how goodbye isn't smart
of love

   —Mark Statman

The Night in Puerto Rico

The night in
  Puerto Rico
   is very dark
Sometimes it is cool
  and sometimes
   chill

Sometimes if you
  live next to the pond
    you can hear a frog
    or toad croaking
In the *campo*
  if you live in a
    place where snakes
    are you can hear them
It feels like they're
  right next to you in bed
And you can hear the
wind blow
  and hit on your window
When I was a child
in Puerto Rico people
said that "*el coco de
    la noche te va comer*"
which means "the monster
of the night will eat
you" but that's only
  if you don't go to
    sleep

And they say that
*el coco de la
  noche* walks around
    and eats people

And when you
  stay awake in the
    night you can hear
    someone walk out
    side and it
      might be "*el
      coco de la noche*"

    —Thairi Soler, sixth grade

I've always had a lot of trouble sleeping. I'm not exactly sure why. Initially, I think it might have had to do with childhood fears, confusion, nightmares. When Thairi Soler handed me her poem and I read it, I practically shivered. It was a story from my own nightmares.

My adult insomnia is harder for me to explain. Sometimes I think it's because sleeping is a time of not doing anything and not knowing what's going on in my life and in the world. In the darkness, everything seems meaningless to me. There's nothing I can do about my life.

My problems with insomnia have caused me to think a lot about dreaming, and that thinking has become a part of my writing and teaching. What are dreams? Where do dreams come from? What do they mean? When talking with younger students about dreams, I present a simple model for how to think about dreams, what they are and why we have them. I tell the students that good dreams are things we want to happen that may or may not be possible (I want to write poetry, I want to be able to breathe underwater). Bad dreams are things that we don't want to happen but can (My bicycle is getting rusty). Nightmares are things that we don't want to happen and that can't happen (All the kids in the class have claws and gargoyle heads and breathe dragon fire).

So good dreams advise us of our desires. They let our subconscious minds work out our longings: we find out more about what we find fantastic and entertaining and we learn more of our own hopes, aspirations, and wants.

Our bad dreams also advise us. The bad dream about my bicycle's rusting away or a bad dream about failing a test or being late for the airplane suggest to us that something needs attending to.

Time to check the bike.

Time to study.

Did I set the alarm? Pack everything? Got the tickets?

Our nightmares can vividly show us what we fear. Oddly enough, they also can be a kind of entertainment. My students like horror movies not because they like to be scared, but because they like the thrilling relief they feel when they realize that what has scared them is not real, that in fact, everything is fine and under control even though, only seconds before, everything had been frightening. Nightmares can work in the same way: kids don't like having them at the moment, but they do like having *had* them. Often they talk about them with great pleasure.

Of course, a good dream, a bad dream, and a nightmare can all occur in one dream.

These three definitions may not be clinically accurate, but they work for younger children. And when I teach them, it helps me explain what I mean by "dream poems." I've had to make the dream versus nightmare description explicit because for a while I was getting too many Freddy

Krueger (from the *Nightmare on Elm Street* movie series) poems. Actually, some of them were fun:

> Freddy Krueger sees
> the spring
> He sees the clouds and girls
> He hears rap songs
> oh yeah oh yeah oh
> He likes to kiss the girls
> but the girls are scared
> of him
>
>   *—Claude Reed, first grade*

But I want the kids to move beyond *Elm Street.* I want them to think about their dreams as straddling the line between the imaginary and the possible. In fact, what I want them to do is not just remember their dreams. I want them to wonder about them. I tell them the story of how when my son Jesse was forty-five minutes old, he was asleep in my arms. I looked at his tiny shut eyelids and saw he was having rapid eye movements. Scientists tell us that in sleep these indicate that we're dreaming. But what does a forty-five-minute-old infant dream? What language does he use to think of what is going on in his tiny head, in this new sleep?

Sometimes, I'll hand out the following poem of mine:

A Dream

Sleeping
I hear music, soft,
and I see that I am underwater
breathing, not drowning
there are millions of fish
green and gold and blue
A green tree asks me my name
I say, I can't remember
The tree laughs
It gives me a sweet red apple
Don't be afraid, it says
Be happy
You can wake up whenever you want to

What's happening here? I ask.
You're having a dream.

And what happens?

They talk about the music, the breathing underwater. Someone notices that there's something a little scary in the poem.

What is it?

That you can't remember your name.

Why is that scary?

Because it would be scary if you couldn't remember who you are.

So is this a nightmare?

No.

Why?

Because the tree takes care of you. He says not to worry and he gives you an apple.

What else?

He tells you how to get out of the dream. He tells you you can wake up when you want to. That means you're in control.

I turn the questions back to them. What do they dream about? What do they remember of their dreams? What do they want and not want? Some students say that they don't have dreams or that they don't remember their dreams. I tell them, though, that dreaming is not just something that happens at night. We have daydreams, those moments of pretending to be paying attention to the teacher when really the mind is miles away, at the beach or in the mountains. I talk about hopes and wishes and remind them that Martin Luther King, Jr.'s "I have a dream" was about the future. I tell them they can also write about a dream that they might like to have, one that would be perfect for their sleep. I tell them that the key to the success of their poem is in describing their dreams so clearly that the reader has the experience—the joy, the strangeness, the fear—they had.

> This is dirty grass
> and it looks like snow
> I'm looking for a tree, looking
> for a tree
> I must go to sleep
> Looking for a monster
> Looking in my room, see
> Looking in my dreams, see
> Looking in my house, no
> Looking in my mouth, no
> Looking at my doctor

The doctor's going to wash my teeth
Says go back home
Looking for my mother
I forgot my mother

    —Tawona, kindergarten

When I am sleeping
in the bed
I hear rain
I hear wind
I hear people
walking home

    —Ismail Abdur, kindergarten

My mountain is a sleep mountain
I like to go to sleep
I'm not going to let nobody
wake me up
or they'll fall off
the mountain
But if my mother wakes me up
I will kiss her

    —Alicia Millington, first grade

Yo sueño que ando
descansando en el cielo y
al mísmo tiempo hablando
con los pajaros
no son 8
no son 90
son millones
de pajaros unos son
chiquitos y unos estan
en mis manos
y una rana saliendo del agua
para volar con los pajaros
y yo y un gato
despertando al perico
para que lo lleve a volar
con los pajaros

I dream that I walk
resting in the sky and

at the same time talking
with the birds
there aren't 8
there aren't 90
there are millions
of birds. Some are
small and some are
in my hands
and a frog is leaving the water
to fly with the birds
and I and a cat
waking the parrot
so that it can take it to fly
with the birds

    —Juan Hernandez, first grade

yo sueño que
yo estoy en el cielo
viendo la estrella
el sol y la luna
en la noche cantan las estrellas
para dormirme
y en el sol está mi nombre
y en la luna está el nombre
de mi hermana

I dream that
I am in the sky
seeing a star
the sun and the moon
in the night the stars sing
me to sleep
and in the sun is my name
and in the moon is the name
of my sister

    —Jasmine Tigre, third grade

When I fall asleep, I almost always
dream about tall trees. I sit on the
ground painting the trees and
the trees come down and ask me if
I need any help. Sometimes the trees
and I sing songs and play games and

everything but the dream always
ends the same way. The people next to
the forest forget to put out their
fire and the trees burn.

    —*Phillip E. Frazier, fourth grade*

II. Dreaming, Part Two: The Animals

When teaching dream poems, I've found it possible, in particular when working with older kids, to extend the discussion about dreaming and to have them think about dreams that have little to do with their own. Margaret Atwood's "Dreams of the Animals" is a good example of how one poet has done this.

Dreams of the Animals

Mostly the animals dream
of other animals   each
according to its kind

    (though certain mice and small rodents
     have nightmares of a huge pink
     shape with five claws descending)

: moles dream of darkness and delicate
mole smells

frogs dream of green and golden
frogs
sparkling like wet suns
among the lilies
red and black
striped fish, their eyes open
have red and black striped
dreams   defense, attack, meaningful
patterns

birds dream of territories
enclosed by singing.

Sometimes the animals dream of evil
in the form of soap and metal
but mostly the animals dream
of other animals.

There are exceptions:

> the silver fox in the roadside zoo
> dreams of digging out
> and of baby foxes, their necks bitten
>
> the caged armadillo
> near the train
> station, which runs
> all day in figure eights
> its piglet feet pattering,
> no longer dreams
> but is insane when waking;
>
> the iguana
> in the petshop window on St Catherine Street
> crested, royal-eyed, ruling
> its kingdom of water-dish and sawdust
>
> dreams of sawdust.

This poem has been a particular favorite with a number of the teachers with whom I've worked. Many have asked me specifically, year after year, to teach it in their classes. Others have been so drawn to the possibilities of the poem, though, that they've actually asked me *not* to teach it: they want to do it themselves.

There's a lot going on in "Dreams of the Animals." I like Margaret Atwood's line breaks, the way the poem looks on the page, the way the poet's sense of space becomes part of the sense and meaning of the poem. Seeing the word *moles* under *moles* and *frogs* under *frogs* creates a kind of visual meter. Each individual line with its individual image gives us a single picture. But it combines with succeeding lines to create another, another, and another, giving us the experience of the whole poem, as well as its many parts: "green and golden / frogs / sparkling like wet suns / among the lilies." Here the sky is brought to the water. And in the form of a frog.

I enjoy Atwood's playfulness with perception. Contrary to what humans might think, frogs see frogs as beautiful. Moles (which smell pretty awful) think of their scents as "delicate."

The final dreams are riveting. The silver fox dreams of a freedom it will never have. Its future at best is as a fur coat or stole. The armadillo no longer has dreams, hopes, or desires. And, having lost the ability to dream, it has gone insane. Meanwhile, the iguana, an animal worshipped by some cultures, dreams of nothing more than sawdust.

A question I often ask the kids is, who has it the worst? Is it the one that dreams of a freedom it will never have? The one that can't dream at all but doesn't even know it can't? Or is it the one that, once considered a god, dreams of something almost valueless, and even sadder, only of what it already has? Of course, there are no right answers. But the ensuing discussion is always interesting.

Before the students write their own Dreams of the Animals poems, I ask them to think about the different kinds of animals that interest them and why (sometimes I ask them, *before* we read the Atwood poem, to write the names of these animals on a piece of paper; that way they already have animals to think about, although I let them know they're not restricted to these animals and don't have to write about any of them if there are other animals that appeal to them more). I remind them that the point is to imagine and write down the dreams that the animals might really have. This means thinking about what the animal, if it could speak or write, would care about, as opposed to what a human, who might have been transformed into that animal, might care about. An eagle, for example, unaware of the existence of a hamburger, would surely not dream of flying to Burger King. But it might dream of trout in a stream on a summer day. If the students want to go beyond dreams and into nightmares for the animals, I let them know that this is all right.

There is a blue horse
on a hill
His owner didn't want him
He misses the fields
The chicken
The barn
and all the things in the farm
He is on a trail to another farm
He is in Colorado
eating grass

   —*Omar Reyes, third grade*

Snake's Dream and Rat

The snake dreams about
      rats

      catching
      rats
When a snake catches a rat it
is
      happy
But what about the rat it feels
sad
      eaten
            chewed up
Dead as a doornail
But it is the snake's dream
But when the rat dreams it
probably is dreaming about being a giant
      and
      killing snakes
      scaring snakes
wanting to do what the snake
does to the rat. But then the snake
      feels
            sad
                  eaten up
                  chewed up
      dead as a doornail
But this is the rat's dream
And the rat is happy
But when the snake is up
and the rat is up
Snatch!
The snake has breakfast

    —*Jon Kappel, sixth grade*

Giraffe

The young giraffe
dreams
of being able to
reach the leaves on the
tall acacia trees of
the land
The giraffe
that has no mother
must eat shrubs from
the hot African floor
He cannot reach the green
moist leaves but must eat

the dry brown shrubs
in order to stay alive
The young giraffe must
run with
no mother to protect him
But soon the shrubs
are gone and the
giraffe is no longer
short and able to reach
the leaves he is free

　　—*Matthew Guevara, sixth grade*

Chapter 9

Seeing Ourselves in the World

I. Identity: What Do You Want Me to Know about You?

Life Harbor

what you get
is a beginning
middle and
time on earth
a kind of story
but the simplicity
of that description
won't wash
because the box
the life gets put in
has a top and bottom
but no sides
and so all the things
that happen to you
keep spilling out
so much of
who I am
connecting to who you are
that my story
has you in it
and I'm in yours
watching out for so many
rhythms
the drums that keep
insisting
I know their language
when all I really know
is their sound

　　—*Mark Statman*

I read my own poetry to try to understand myself. I look at what I've said, thought, and done, and try to figure out how and why I did those things. I try to figure out what effect—with all the "spilling" and "connecting"—my language and actions have had on others.

When I work with students, I often ask them to do the same kind of thing. I ask them to talk and write about who they are, about how they understand themselves and how connected or disconnected they feel with or from the world. Their ability to do this takes some time to develop because often the complications of their identities aren't clear to them. Finding that clarity requires time for reflection, which their lives usually don't provide. Allowing writing time in their lives creates space for that kind of thinking.

When I begin working with a group of students, I try to learn as much about them as possible. I want them to learn about me, too. I introduce myself as Mark, and I write that one word on the chalkboard. Then I walk around the room asking each student to tell me his or her first name. As each does, I repeat the name, then repeat the names of some of those who have already introduced themselves. This goes on until everyone has spoken, a lot of fun because it gets a little crazy as I swing through the classroom, sometimes making mistakes as the number of names increases, sometimes needing someone to say his or her name several times. Occasionally the students have name tags that they bring out for visitors. But fortunately I have the ability to learn a lot of names quickly, so I say to them, No, no, no, I don't want to *read* your names, I want to meet *you*.

Having done this, I point out that although I've learned their names, I don't really know them as people. And they know my name, but they don't know anything about me. They don't know where I live, what I like, what I don't, my favorite sports, my favorite teams. They don't know about my family or friends. In fact, I ask them, does a name tell us anything at all?

Of course not, they reply, although occasionally a student might point out that a name can indicate gender, but even that's something we realize we can't be certain of.

I then point out to them that many names do have specific meanings, that there are name dictionaries. I talk about how before my son's birth, I got interested in those meanings. I tell them how we found out that my son Jesse's name means one who is blessed. I note that my wife Katherine's name means pure. Then I tell them of a friend named Alex who told me his name means brave. Another friend's name, Michael, means gift of God. Finally, I tell them about Raymond, whose name, from the Spanish *rey* and *mundo*, means king of the world. As I talk, I write these names and their meanings on the board.

The students are often excited about all this. And what, they ask, since my name is also on the board but with no meaning next to it, does Mark mean?

With this question, I sigh. I ask them what they know about the Romans. Sometimes they can tell me quite a bit. If they know nothing, I talk about the powerful empire that existed centuries ago. I mention how even to this day we feel the influence of the Romans in our lives. For example, I point out, they affected how astronomers named the planets in our solar system. Many of the students are familiar with the Roman gods and goddesses.

And what's the biggest planet in the solar system? I ask.

Jupiter.

And who was the chief god?

Jupiter.

That's right, I respond, because, after all, where else would the chief god live, but on the biggest planet?

We go through some more planets: the oceanic-looking planet would be the perfect place for the god of the oceans, Neptune. The fastest planet around the sun would be named for the fast messenger god, Mercury. The planet that shines so beautifully in the sky that it is often confused for a star would be named for Venus, the goddess of love. Distant Pluto gets its name for the god of the underworld.

And then, I say, there's the red planet in the sky. Red, which is like blood, which comes from killing, from war.

Mars! they shout out.

I write the words *blood, killing, war* under my name. I circle the Mar of Mark. The chalkboard now looks like this:

Mark	Jesse—blessed
blood	Katherine—pure
killing	Alex—brave
war	Michael—beloved of God
	Raymond—king of the world

113

There's some giggling now, some talking. What, I ask, do you think my problem is? I get many answers.

You don't like your name.

Those names are good, your name isn't.

Your name isn't you.

So what, I ask, should I do?

Change your name, is the inevitable reply.

Oh, come on, I say, I can't change my name. I've had this name for too long. It's how people know me. It's what my parents named me. But if I don't like the meaning of my name and I can't change my name, what can I change?

The meaning, someone guesses.

Exactly, I say.

But many of the students are unsure. How can we change meanings of words?

I'm a poet, I say, smiling, I can do anything. And with that I hand out the following poem.*

My Name

In the dictionary
it says
Mark means
the Roman god of war
someone who likes to fight
except
I hate to fight

The dictionary is wrong
Mark means
someone who likes to write
It means
I like the color blue
beautiful blue skies
and blue oceans

---

* Obviously, I've built this lesson around the unsavory derivation of *my* name, but even if you don't know the meaning of your name, or if your name means something terrific, you can still do a lesson like this. The point here is to give kids a sense of the authority of what they know about themselves. When the kids read their poems, I always ask the listeners if they've learned anything new on hearing a classmate's work. Usually, they (and their teachers) have, much to the delight, and sometime surprise, of the poet.

Mark means
the one who likes to sleep late
the one who likes to dream
the one who rides his mountain bike
in the green cool woods
Mark means
I have a son named Jesse
I have thousands of books
I hate when it gets too cold
and I want to go to Mexico
Mark means
let's have fun
let's tell jokes
let's pretend the world is crazy

And those are only some of the things
I know Mark means

　—*Mark Statman*

We read the poem. Now, I ask, what do you really know about me? The students respond with all the details of the poem. Do you know a lot more than before? I ask.

Yes.

I tell them to do for me what I've done for them. I ask them to write a poem that talks about who they really are, that isn't what someone else might necessarily say—not their parents, teachers, friends, or a name book—but how they understand themselves. Tell me what you like, I say, what you hate. Tell me what makes you happy, what makes you mad, scared, sad. Tell me what you think I ought to know about who you are, things I'd never guess just by hearing your name or seeing your face.

When they write, some of the students do this by using the name model I've offered. Others just describe themselves, sometimes by telling about significant moments in their lives.*

---

* With my first-semester college students, I take a different approach to this poem of identity. In past years, my students have complained that all of their seminar classes seem to begin the first day in the same way: "Say something about who you are, where you're from, why you came to this college." This might prove useful to the instructor, but many students find it tedious. So I ask them to write acrostics on their names, letting us know something different or personal about themselves. I model one:

My Name

My name means good
not bad it means
someone who likes to play I don't like
the
    cold
so to Dominican
Republic I want to
go I could not like the
    cold
but I do like
the
    snow
My favorite color
is white because it is
part of the
    sky
I like to pretend
that I am the queen
that I fly on the
sky with beautiful
    wings

   —Veranda Sanchez, fourth grade

Corey

My name is a
feeling

      Mornings I like to sleep
      lAte and dream until I end up
downstairs Reading the newspaper while Jesse
      and Katherine eat breakfast

Here I've given them a few things to think about—my family, my sleeping habits, where I might live, the kind of casual quality I like my life to have (and too often doesn't!).

The acrostic works for the college students because it's a form they know but usually associate with elementary school. For some reason, this association makes the writing of the acrostic seem slightly silly, but that fact seems to give them the space to be less personally or literarily self-conscious and more open, funny, and honest than if I'd asked them to write a "poem" about "who you are."

A feeling of hope
love happiness and
laughter
My name is a
paper and pencil
just waiting to be used
My name is a gallant horse
Striding freely across a
meadow
My name can be lonely
Sad and blue
It can change like night
and day
It loves to talk and sing
and be the star of the
show
There is more though
So much more
but all other things
I have yet to explore

    —Corey Bindler, fifth grade

I like bumblebees
I like sunny days
I like pepperoni pizza
I like playing baseball
My favorite team is the Mets
I like my house
because it has my bed
and something to eat and
a refrigerator
I like wood on a tree
because if it's cold you
get fire

    —Stephen Luczaj, kindergarten

I like my house
I like the tulip with pollen in it
I like the way I have green bushes
around my door
I do not like the worm
I like McDonald's
I don't like a bird on the window

I like a balloon
and I like a rainbow

  —*Robbie Torosian, kindergarten*

When I Was Born

When
I was
born
I entered
a world
where I
could
do
anything
I want
When
I was
born
I thought
to
myself
God
has given
me
a gift
to see
to hear
to touch
to taste
and
to feel
anything
I want
When
I was
born
I
looked around
and
I saw
stuff

I
never
saw before
I heard
stuff
I
never
heard before
I touched
stuff
I never
tasted before
When
I was
born
I
looked up
and
I
saw
an angel
waving
hello
to me
then
waving good-bye
because
I was
leaving
the place
I'd been
before
and
entering
a whole
new place
because
I was born

    —Samrah Naseem, fifth grade

Me

Me, who laughs at the clouds
who smiles at the sky
who adores books
has theories
Nature is a gift
Loves being wild, zany
absolutely insane
tries new things
spreads my wings
explores the unlimited world
of possibilities
Freckles run across my face
my blue eyes dance and twinkle
Cats are soft; I like them
Frogs are slimy; I like them
light blue flowers tucked in hair
sweet, like me

—*Lexi Merwin, fifth grade*

II. Identification: Finding Yourself Elsewhere

The Negro Speaks of Rivers

I've known rivers:
I've seen rivers ancient as the world and older than the
    flow of human blood in human veins.

My soul has grown deep like the rivers.

I bathed in the Euphrates when dawns were young.
I built my hut near the Congo and it lulled me to sleep.
I looked upon the Nile and raised the pyramids above it.
I heard the singing of the Mississippi when Abe Lincoln
    went down to New Orleans, and I've seen its muddy
    bosom turn all golden in the sunset.

I've known rivers:
Ancient, dusky rivers.

My soul has grown deep like the rivers.

—*Langston Hughes*

In "The Negro Speaks of Rivers," Langston Hughes gives us a powerful sense of what happens when you move from thinking about your identity (who you are) and begin to think about identification (how you see yourself in relation to others). In a session that might follow the name lesson, I ask the kids to think about this. Sometimes I'll start with Hughes: Who do the students think he is? Why does he speak of rivers? We talk about how his identification with others like him has deepened his soul, allowed him to see the power that comes from seeing oneself with others.

I ask the kids how they understand their own identities and whom they might identify with. We talk about different people we might identify with because of what we do, what we like or don't like, and how, by making identifications, we're able to see how we're like others and how we are different.

One way I do this is to ask everyone to raise his or her hand. I raise mine as well. I ask all those who are human beings to keep a hand up (all stay). Okay, I say, we all can identify with each other as human beings. Then I continue: All human beings who like pizza, keep your hands up. Most stay up. I note then for the students that most of us can still identify with each other. The students look around, nodding.

Now, I go on, all human beings who like pizza and think the color blue is one of their top three colors, keep your hand up. Many remain. I add, Who also like baseball. Fewer now. Who are also male. Now it's just the boys and me. Who speak Spanish. At this point, depending on the school and its population, there might be five or six hands up, there might be one or two. I'm still one of them. Then I say, Who are also fathers. At that point, I'm left alone.

What we've done, I explain, is to show how identity and identification show what we have in common but also what we don't. I note how most of us could connect as pizza-lovers, but there was no one with whom I could connect as a father.

This leads to a final question for them: Are our identities and identifications always conscious and freely chosen? The clear answer is no. There's little free choice in being human, or in our race or gender. We might choose to like pizza, although even that's tricky—do we train our own taste buds? Sports and colors seem a little bit more conscious. That

I speak Spanish is a choice, but, as many students easily note, it would not be if I lived in a country where Spanish is the primary language.

There are also varied ways of understanding one's identity and identification. Identity can be described by gender, by class, or by race, for example. And these do often get named by the students and discussions emerge around what it means to be male or female, white, African American, Latino, rich, poor, and so on. It seems essential to me that we talk about these things with the students, at least with older ones for whom these categories are becoming issues.

In talking about identity with the students, I hope that they'll think about their own individuality. The question, again, is not simply how others might label you, but how you label yourself. And what does it mean that you have chosen to describe yourself this way, and what then does that say about your own sense of identification with others?*

In a simple way, for example, as a baseball fan, I can easily identify with other baseball fans, but more so with fans who are fans of my favorite team, and less so with fans of the opposition. I identify with other parents, but usually I have more in common with the fathers than the mothers. I identify with other poets, but not so much with performance poets as with poets who work on the page. The more I attempt to describe myself, the more the complexities, complications, and limitations of different identities and identifications arise. I am a white male who lives in New York City: it would be ridiculous for me to think that this fact has no effect on how I understand the world. It would be ridiculous for me to think that, being who I am, I could easily understand the point of view, needs, and wants of someone who is quite different from me. Which isn't to say that I *can't* do it. In fact, it's one of the things that being imaginative and writing creatively allows us to try. But the fact is, it isn't easily done, and requires a lot of serious thinking.†

Having talked about identity and identification, I tell the students the story of Gabriela Mistral, the Chilean poet who was the first Latin American to win the Nobel Prize for Literature, and whose work we're going

---

* A powerful essay on the subject of identity is Adrienne Rich's "Split at the Root: An Essay in Jewish Identity."

† This isn't to say that, in my being different, my knowledge, needs, and wants automatically become different as well. Too often, identity has been used to make distinctions between people, at the cost of seeing what people might still have in

to look at (right away, I point out all the different "identities" we've estab-lished—woman, Chilean, poet, Latin American winner of the Nobel, object of study). I tell them how, in fact, Gabriela Mistral is not the poet's given name, that she was born Lucila Godoy y Alcayaga. I tell them how when Lucila was growing up, nobody thought much of her. Her teachers thought she was slow, uninterested, and uninteresting. They told Lucila's mother that school wasn't the place for her (it wasn't mandatory) and they predicted that her future would be that of a house servant. But Lucila badly wanted to be a teacher. After she was asked to leave a number of dif-ferent schools, her mother and stepsister, who were both teachers, decided that they'd teach her at home. By the time she was fifteen, she was working as a teacher's assistant; at twenty-one, she was a high school teacher. Lucila became such a wonderful teacher and such an innovator in progressive teaching that the president of Chile named her "Teacher of the Nation." She became an international figure in educational reform, consulting in the United States, Mexico, Brazil, Italy, France, and England.

But that isn't the whole Lucila story, I tell the students. In her mid-teens, Lucila began writing poetry. She published her poems in local newspapers and magazines, signing them "A Friend" and "Someone." However, in 1914, when she was twenty-five, she decided to enter her country's national poetry contest. To do so, she had to give a name, but since it wouldn't seem proper for a young schoolteacher to be writing such passionate poems, Lucila realized she needed a pen name, one that would go along with her identity as a poet.

She chose Gabriela Mistral. Gabriela came from the archangel Gabriel, the opponent of evil. The mistral is a cold north wind that blows over the Mediterranean coast of France and nearby regions. So here was her identity: Gabriela Mistral, the poet. And her identification: her poetry would be a fierce wind against evil.

Mistral, I tell the students, actually did go on to win the poetry con-test. It was the beginning of one of the great poetic careers of this cen-tury. The lesson? I ask. Hands come up.

---

common. But the point here is in the *assumption* that I know someone else sim-ply because I have a good idea of what I know about myself. Not only shouldn't I assume I know others, in fact, I *must* not. And that's part of the point of talking with the students about identity and identification: it helps them to become aware of what they know about themselves. It also gets them to think about what they *don't* know about themselves.

Don't let anyone ever tell you you're stupid, or that you can't do something if you really want to.

Why?

Because if it is what you want, you have to try.

What if it's someone who's supposed to know better, I respond, a grown-up, a teacher?

That doesn't make that person right.

Exactly, I say. Imagine what would have happened to Gabriela Mistral if Lucila had listened to all those other people and not herself.

There wouldn't have been a Gabriela Mistral.

Exactly. Then I hand out the following poem.

Ayudadores

Mientras el niño se me duerme,
sin que lo sepa ni la tierra,
por ayudarme en acabarlo
sus cabellos hace la hierba,
sus deditos la palma-dátil
y las uñas la buena cera.
Los caracoles dan su oído
y la fresa roja su lengua,
el arroyo le trae risas
y el monte le manda paciencias.

(Cosas dejé sin acabar
y estoy confusa y con vergüenza:
apenas sienes, apenas habla,
apenas bulto que le vean.)

Los que acarrean van y vienen,
entran y salen por la puerta
trayendo orejitas de *cuye*
y unos dientes de concha-perla.

Tres Navidades y será otro,
de los tobillos a la cabeza:
será talludo, será recto
como los pinos de la cuesta.

Y yo, iré entonces voceándolo
como una loca por los pueblos,
con un pregón que van a oírme
las praderías y los cerros.

—*Gabriela Mistral*

The Helpers

While my baby sleeps
neither he nor the earth knows
how the earth helps me complete him.
The grass makes his hair,
his fingers, the date palm
and his fingernails come from beeswax.
Seashells give him his hearing,
and the red strawberry his tongue,
the stream carries his laughter
and the mountain sends him patience.

(I've left so much undone
and I am confused, ashamed:
almost no forehead, almost no voice,
almost too small to see.)

Those that carry these go and come,
enter and leave through the door
bringing little guinea pig ears
and teeth of mother-of-pearl.

Three Christmases and he'll be another
from head to toe:
He'll be grown, grown straight
like the pines on the slope.

And I will go then, through the towns
a crazy woman, proclaiming him
with a cry heard
by the meadows and hills.

What's going on? I ask.
Her baby isn't done.*
What does that mean?
When babies are born, the students answer, they're not whole people
yet. They're all squished up. They have to be finished.
So how does the baby in this poem get finished?
By nature, they reply. By the earth.

---

* Interestingly, Mistral never had children, but she loved them greatly and considered her students as her own, creating for herself another kind of identity/identification.

We talk about how this happens. Date palm leaves look like fingers, baby fingernails are soft, like beeswax, seashells have ear shapes and the sound of the ocean in them. Our tongues look like strawberies, both in color and shape. One fourth grader noted, too, that strawberries are sweet and that's the best taste for the tongue.

Why, I ask, in the second verse, is she confused and ashamed? A hard question, but some students have ideas.

Because it's her baby. It isn't finished, but she feels like it's her responsibility. She needs to do her job and she isn't sure she has.

And what about the three Christmases? I continue. This is a tough question, too, but soon the answers come. Sometimes from the students, sometimes from the teacher.

In three Christmases, the baby is three, almost four years old. The baby isn't a baby anymore. It will keep growing, but already a lot of who the child will be is clear.

I ask the students about younger brothers, sisters, or cousins: does any of this seem true for children they know? It does.

Identity: who you are. Identification: how you are in connection or relation to others. Mistral identifies her baby with gifts from nature. Write poems, I say, about your identity and identification. Some students decide to do it the way Mistral does, focusing on how nature completes them. For others, the focus is like Hughes's: the identification is not so much how the world is part of them, but more how they see themselves in connection—and disconnection—to it.

I'm the Lake

I am the lake
I am the one
that splashes in
the night, I am
the one that moves
smooth in the
morning, I am
the one that
makes the swan
move, I am the
one that makes
big waves in the
rain. When it is

nice and calm I make
soft waves. I can
see the trees in
my reflection

    —Krystal Cummins, third grade

Mi Inspiración

El sol es mi inspiración
    para seguir adelante
Dos bolítas cafes hacen mis ojos

Mi alegría viene del aíre puro
La palma de mi mano
es como una hoja nueva
Mis lagrimas son como un pétalo
de rosa que se cae

The sun is my inspiration
to go forward
Two little brown balls are my eyes
My happiness comes from the pure air
The palm of my hand
is like a new leaf
My tears are like
a falling rose petal

    —Carmen Santos, fifth grade

If my eyes are the stars that stare
down at earth

Then my hands are the soil, how
much am I worth?

If my hairs are the feathers
that catch the cool breeze,

Is my tongue so sharp, that
I sting like a bee?

How much can you pay for
a glimpse of a free butterfly?

It's priceless, you see, like
the sea and the sky.

My skin is mud, gentle and
smooth

And my fingers use dirt in
a gentle groove.

 —Allison Sepe, sixth grade

One day
I was in the grass
The sun came out
I felt happy
I felt like a princess

 —Anne Palmiotto, first grade

I am . . .

I am a turquoise star shimmering
in the dark night
I am a dolphin leaping
out of the blue Florida ocean
I am a bird singing
my favorite song in a dogwood tree
I am thunder talking
to the wild animals in the forest
I am a rocking chair rocking
a baby back and forth
I am happiness hiding
nervously behind a dark desolate eye
I am

 —Jenna M. Schmidt, sixth grade

The Days before the Grave

When I do nothing, the trees will grow
Life will go on outside my world
People will die and flowers will wilt
Dark thoughts will be thought and I will still sit
Days will die and nights will begin
People will cry and I will still sit
People will laugh and people will sing
and I will still have thoughts that I cannot think
People will wallow in their own selves, despise

Pure red hatred will burn through their eyes
People will laugh and I will still sit

    —Sari Zeidler, sixth grade

Chilled but Free

As I am at my window, sitting chilled and cold.
An eagle.
A bird.
Wings.
Flying away on his problems.
Never ending the beginnings.
Like the wind.
As I am at my window I look and compare.
A carefree bird.
Free.
The whole way through.
As a chill comes through my window
—evidence of the free bird's fall—
an enchanting free feather.
Give me wings.
Give me wings.
I will go on.

    —Caitlin Gallagher, fifth grade

I like the way apples taste
and the way butterflies fly
My best friend is Abigail
because she's nice
Strawberry ice cream is my favorite
Adam is nice and kind
That's why he's my friend

    —Theresa Groves, kindergarten

I Would Like To

I would like to know
what nothing is
To understand how dying feels
without really trying
I would like to find
what I can do
What I can do to fight

without really fighting
I would like to see
a fairy in her garden
And to know
what to do to become
who I am
I would like to be
a raindrop
for one moment
To feel millions of
years old
to feel water
being who I am
For just a moment
I would like to be able
to go back in time
do something over
Make things better
I would like to
see the rain
fall below me
I would like to
live a life

  —*Helen Staab, fifth grade*

III. Biography: Writing out of History

Power

Living   in the earth-deposits   of our history

Today a backhoe divulged   out of a crumbling flank of earth
one bottle   amber   perfect   a hundred-year-old
cure for fever   or melancholy   a tonic
for living on this earth   in the winters of this climate

Today I was reading about Marie Curie:
she must have known she suffered   from radiation sickness
her body bombarded for years   by the element
she had purified
It seems she denied to the end
the source of the cataracts on her eyes
the cracked and suppurating skin   of her finger-ends
till she could no longer hold   a test-tube or a pencil

> She died   a famous woman   denying
> her wounds
> denying
> her wounds   came   from the same source as her power
>
> —*Adrienne Rich*

Adrienne Rich's "Power" is a poem I often teach to older elementary school students who have been looking at the lives of important historical figures. It can help broaden the process of connecting with things and places they started with their identification poems.

When we read "Power," I ask the kids about the Marie Curie they see in the poem. I ask them to think about what power is and what the poet means by it, and to think about the meaning of what Curie does, how her power as a scientist and a thinker also requires that she ignore the wounds caused by the radium even as she purifies the substance. In talking about what radium is and what it has meant to our world—it has had significant use in cancer therapies—we often move to a broader, more general discussion of radioactive materials. I ask them to think about the positives and the negatives: uses of radiation in war, in medicine, as a "clean" energy source versus polluting energy sources, the problems of nuclear waste. I ask them to think about the relationship of the second verse to the "tonic" of the first. We talk about tonics as fake cures, the idea of the snake-oil salesman trying to sell you something worthless. Certainly the radium Curie purifies is not fake, and Curie's work clearly benefits others, but it also kills her. I ask the students to think again, what do they think of what Marie Curie did? Was the exercise of her power worth the result?

Rich's poem also has a way of making a historical figure more human. Often students will know that Marie Curie was A Great Woman Scientist (as they'll know that George Washington was The Father of Our Country and Abraham Lincoln was The President Who Freed the Slaves). But the idea that these Great People were more than that—that they were people with real lives, who were happy and sad, who fell in love, and ate dinner—isn't usually a part of a young person's historical thinking. It should be, though, because by making historical figures more personal, students are able to understand them better. The students can see similarities between themselves and those figures, and thus see themselves as part of history. In this way, history doesn't seem remote and irrelevant.

When I ask the kids to use the personal lives of historic figures in their writing, I urge them to internalize those lives, to *become* those figures so they can write from that point of view. I ask them to think about moments in the biography of the person that stand out as different or unusual or surprising. I suggest that they write about a private moment, one that might be connected with our knowledge of the figure's fame but doesn't have to be. I remind them that even though they are writing these poems from the point of view of a famous person, they can write them just as they would write about their own lives. Such an approach allows fifth grader Joe Covelli to wonder about the loneliness of Alexander Graham Bell, to examine his famous experiments in the context of his private sadness. It allows Brittany Fiorino to explain what drove Dickens to write as much as he did.

Alexander Graham Bell at Night

I am lonely
I am wondering
I am thinking
I wonder if/or not to wed
I am thinking about my experiment
What will it be?
How will people react?
At night, I am all bottled up
I am sad
because I have no one to talk to
At night I think and wonder
about tomorrow, its reactions and its sorrows
At night I am worried because I may not awaken
When day comes, I will still wonder,
think and be lonely
For when night comes, I will feel the same lonely
thinking, wondering self I
was the night before

  —*Joe Covelli, fifth grade*

Charles Dickens:
I Do It All for Maria

Maria
I do it all for Maria
I'm cold for Maria
I live for Maria

I lived with Maria
I'm poor but not for Maria
I published books not for the money
for Maria
I became wealthy and well known
because of and for Maria
I had children with Maria
Maria died
My heart died with Maria
I can't live without Maria
I do it all for Maria
Maria

    —*Brittany Fiorino, fifth grade*

Chapter 10

Waiting, Hoping, Returning: Some Thoughts on Writing and Teaching

I. This Nervous Feeling

School

When you're on vacation
from school it's exciting!
On vacation I play games
and play outside
But inside of you
you kind of want
to go back
because you miss your teacher
classroom and stuff like that
But when you go back
you have this nervous feeling
don't you?

—Nicole Krakoff, first grade

Every August, I get Nicole's nervousness. Even though I'm still on vacation, trying to relax, write, spend time with my family, maybe travel a little, the school year begins to make its presence known. I get phone calls from school principals and PTA liaisons, about how we need to talk about setting up a teaching schedule. On the college level, letters arrive from the dean's office, reminding me about book orders, library reserves, and academic orientation. I begin to look through my journals from previous years: what poems did I teach, how did it go? I peek at last year's syllabi, thinking about how to revise them. What do I want to do this semester? Any new poems to teach? What will work for the kindergartners, for fifth graders, for college students? What do I expect to happen?

I've begun waiting. Which is hard, because once I start to think about this stuff, I begin to want to do it. I begin to want to go back to my office, then walk out and over to my classroom, and step inside. But I can't do this. I imagine new student faces, notice how composites of old ones make up the new ones. I have imaginary conversations with these students, debates on the merits of an essay we're reading, on one poet or another. We talk about the poems I've been asking them to write, what they're happy about, what they're struggling with. I'm waiting and waiting. More imagined conversation. More debate. Even as I keep my summer schedule, in my head it's fall, red and yellow leaves, then bare branches.

II. Waiting and Hoping: A Lesson

Ayer
los árboles
las flores
y las pequeñas yerbas
se movían
tal vez todavía estén
moviéndose
mientras yo te esperaba
con inquietud
en el parque
temiendo ser sorprendida
por alguien conocido;
pero tú no llegaste
y apareció la noche
ampliamente
aunque lenta
en medio de la gente
que iba y venía
quién sabe a qué dolor
mientras yo allí
parecía una extraña
con una rama
en la mano

　　—*Mayra Jiménez*

Yesterday
the trees
the flowers

135

and the small grasses
they moved
perhaps they still are
moving
while I waited for you
worried
in the park
afraid of being surprised
by someone I knew;
but you didn't come
and the night appeared
grew
though slowly
in the middle of people
who went and came
who knows to what pain
meanwhile there I was
a stranger
with a branch
in my hand

I enjoy teaching this poem by Mayra Jiménez.* My students like it, too. It presents a situation that they can understand. Someone is waiting, hoping (the Spanish word for both is the same, *esperar*), for something to happen. They know what it means to be in the middle of anticipating, the combination of excitement (what they can imagine) and boredom (how slowly the clock moves). They're also interested in the fact that the poet doesn't get what she wants: she's been stood up. She's upset. She doesn't want to be seen by anybody who knows her because she's embarrassed at the idea that someone has done this to her. They understand that she projects her feelings onto everyone around her ("who went and came / who knows to what pain") and they can talk about how they've done that themselves. We also spend a good deal of time talking about how mysterious the last line is. What is that branch in her hand? I once had a student suggest she was going use it to beat up on the person, should the person ever arrive. Others have suggested that it's an olive branch, for

---

* I first met the Venezuelan-born poet, who lives in Costa Rica, in 1987 in Managua, Nicaragua. At the time, along with the poet Ernesto Cardenal, who was Minister of Culture, Mayra was developing and teaching in the Nicaraguan literacy brigades, which used poetry as a way to teach children and adults how to read and write.

reconciliation. Others say that it's the stem of a flower whose petals have all dropped away.

I like to teach this poem, too, because of its attention to language and emotional details. The poem is about waiting and hoping, and about the disappointment that comes with not getting what you've waited and hoped for. The imagery and word choice help create that mood: the grasses are small, nothing is moving, and when the night appears, it does so slowly, drawing out the difficulty of the moment. The trees and flowers have no color, there is nothing beautiful about them. They are separate from the poet, and serve only as one more way for the poet to think about how she feels.

Sometimes I ask the students to imagine the poem Jiménez might have written had the person arrived. What kinds of details might have been used to show happiness, what kinds of colors, what words? I also ask them to think about her use of line length; the skinniness of the poem mirrors the bleakness of it; how would fat lines or a combination of fat and thin, or other kinds of word placements affect the mood?

In their own poems, I ask the students to focus on the time of waiting, and not the time of meeting or receiving. This focus gives them a chance to examine the complexity of the emotions they feel *during* that time. Often—and this is something we talk about—the waiting and hoping time is more physically and emotionally compelling than what comes next. Sometimes (as in the case of Wilbert Miranda's poem below) the idea of waiting and hoping takes the students in directions I couldn't have anticipated.

While I Sat There and Waited

Yesterday it was dark and black
    in the sky

While in my house, I waited
walking angrily

Afraid of telling somebody
    that you have not called
The black trees swing back and
    forth
While I wait angrily for
    you to call
Meanwhile there I was
    a stranger

                    in my own house
My feelings trapped inside of me
        I could not tell you
        how I felt
                    on the phone

    —*Adrienne Ricks, fifth grade*

nosotros somos bebés
después somos mediano
después somos grande
después somos señores
después somos viejito
y después nos morirmos
los dias pasan rápido
como los conejos

we are babies
then we are medium
then we are big
then we are adults
then we are old
and then we die
the days pass quickly
like rabbits

    —*Wilbert Miranda, third grade*

    I waited looking
up at the misty sky. Dawn came
    and took me over the
hills and then
    he took me through the
clouds and up to the moon with
    his gray white coat
I slid down his wing

    —*Ashley Duke, fourth grade*

I play with snow
It is shaped with beauty

You see the people you know
The soup waits to be eaten
It is a perfect time to play
The white glistening snow glistens
through the day

It waits to be played in
Have your snowball fights
Have your fun
To me this is a wonder

    —Christina Pawlowski, third grade

The Letter

Lisette
you left me waiting for you at
the beach
The sand went through my toes
while I walked
I sat on a rock while the sun
was
setting and the birds flying
through
It wasn't like when we were kids
Now you're gone
I hope you write back love you
forever

(I dedicate this poem to my best
friend, Lisette Vasquez)

    —Jahida Rodriguez, fifth grade

Difference/Waiting

There is nothing to do
There is nothing to see
Just a plain wall
No color or form
I hear the thin air
No response

    —Alex Balsam, sixth grade

III. Returning: Questions, Conclusions

poem with an end

the craziness of your dreams
has come out of the
craziness of our time
the winter that isn't winter
the summer that comes
before the spring

or the idea of a world
which has no idea
that there's another way to be
not happy with
the way snow falls out
not happy with
why anything isn't
different anymore

that's where you should go
to questions that
point
to mistakes

—Mark Statman

While I'm waiting for the fall semester to start, I spend some time look-ing for new poems to bring to the schools. Teaching new work challenges me. It makes me think about not just how to teach the poems, but why. Why do I think *this* poem is worth reading? Just because I value it, why do I think a first grader or a college senior will? What I like about this ask-ing is that it helps me renew my sense of purpose. It gets me thinking about why I do this in the first place.

This question intrigues me. After all, I never question why I write. I'm a writer, it's how I identify myself, it's what I do. I could never imag-ine not writing. And whereas I'd like to say the same thing about teach-ing, I know there'd be something false about it. I teach, yes, but, despite the fact that I've been doing it for over half of my life, the truth is that my identification of self and soul as teacher just isn't the same as writer, as novelist, as poet.

Which then leads me to ask myself, if the identification isn't that pro-found, but the commitment to teaching really is there, why do I teach? Of course, it *is* about writing. Rilke, in his *Letters to a Young Poet*, notes that all of us are alone in the world, or, at least, that essentially all of us are solitary. I don't know if this is true—my son's birth gave me a greater sense of communion with others than I ever imagined possible. But I do know that to write and to read creatively requires a kind of solitude, to be with and to try to understand my self in all of its imaginative, critical, emotional, intellectual, and physical capacities. It demands that I know the good and bad of these capacities and of my world, and that I must do this in order to find a way to put all that in the language that best describes what it is I've come to know and understand.

However, being engaged in an activity and a profession that is necessarily solitary does not mean that I am not part of the world, that I can be forgiven for not being actively engaged in it, and that I do not have responsibilities to it. So, when I think about the why of teaching, the first thing that comes to mind is the social. Teaching is the way that, as a writer, I can, in person, show others what I think is so important about writing and why. There's nothing more joyful for me than being in a roomful of people, be they kindergartners or college students, and reading, writing, and talking about poetry. The aesthetic part of me wants everyone to see how great literature is, that it's something to be excited about, to be moved by, made happy or sad, focused or dreamy, or whatever!

The pedagogical part of me also knows that there's a wonderfully simple and direct connection between reading and writing creatively and learning how to (and wanting to learn how to) read and write. And read and write more. And better. When someone feels he or she has a stake in what he or she is reading and writing ("This is about me, this is what I want to know about, this is exciting") then that person will continue to want to do it. Spelling and vocabulary lists, phonics, BASAL readers—for most people, these are desire-to-learn killers. A good book, a good poem, these are the best teaching tools we have.

And that brings me to the final reason I teach. For me, being in the classroom is a political act. I know this is not true for all poets. I know that a major concern in doing creative writing is not that it prepares students for something else, that is to say, to the students' learning something "useful." I know that, in itself, writing creatively, being imaginative, crazy and serious, is enjoyable, and that most often the reward for reading and writing poetry is a moment of pleasure, a moment of insight or inspiration.

However, in being a *teacher* of creative writing, I am helping empower others to help themselves, and that's where the politics does come in. It's true that when you link the aesthetic and the pedagogical together, what you're doing is actually encouraging solitary acts (to write, to read). But the person who does these things, who is able to do them for himself or herself, is someone who has spent time understanding who he or she is and is able to express that: I feel, I know, I want, I need. And this is someone who is able to be both creative and critical, who is better equipped to make choices about his or her life. It's someone who, because of greater self-awareness, is better able, whether as part of a classroom, a community, or our entire society, to transfer that sense of the I into a sense of the we, that is to say, be the individual as citizen, someone who listens, speaks, participates, and acts, consciously and unselfishly.

Admittedly, this is all about hope, what I want to and believe should happen for the kids.* Sometimes I talk with them about it. I ask them what they think of what's happening when I'm in the classroom. A lot of the time they're articulate about liking my presence. They like the freedom I give them to write what they want to in the way they want to. They like being praised for what they do. Some even talk about liking the criticism they receive because they understand that it's constructive; it means their work is being taken seriously.

They're having fun, which is extremely important, even though they're usually working hard. They like the process of creating, both for the product they get and for what it takes to get it. In all this, they know they're becoming better writers.

Does that mean they perceive my lofty social goals? I doubt it. But I believe that the work we're doing—their poetry, my poetry, our discussions—affects my life and their lives, and helps me and them to become better writers, better thinkers, better people. Do they see it? I can't say. I do know that from time to time I run into former students. They talk about the poetry we read and wrote. Sometimes they remember the conversations. Often I ask them if they're still writing poetry. Some say yes, some no. The ones who are writing sometimes talk with me about the importance of what we did togther. The ones who aren't writing don't seem to regret having done the work. All seem to remember the experience happily.

---

* Herbert Kohl, in his marvelous collection of essays, *I Won't Learn from You* (New York: The New Press, 1994), talks about the need for educators to see themselves as "hope-mongerers."

My hope is that some are getting the point of it all—the creativity, the thoughtful, critical consciousness—right then and there, in the moment of reading and writing. And the others? With them, I'm hoping that even if the why of what we've been doing together isn't clear at the moment, they'll figure it out later on down the line.

Coda

The Necessary Art of Revision

ocean

the ocean
    is
sitting
    where
it lay silent
        moving
    smashing against the
    waves
       the
    ocean is the
          line
    you jump in

    a sea of
          blues
the
  ocean's
   silent
    waves
     are
       stairs
   leading to the
color blue
       sky

—Jason Head, fifth grade

Revision is an important part of my work with young writers. Practically every poem of theirs in this book has gone through the process I describe below.* My way of doing revision is extremely hands-on. I do it in two phases.

---

* One of the best books on the subject of revising both fiction and nonfiction is Meredith Sue Willis's *Deep Revision* (New York: Teachers & Writers Collaborative, 1993).

Phase One: Early Drafts

The first phase begins soon after the students have begun their first drafts. Once they've started writing, I walk around the room for a few minutes, answering questions, making sure everyone knows what to do. After that, I move off to the side and let the students work. This is usually a good time, if the teacher isn't actually doing the writing too, to get feedback from him or her on the lesson, to see what the teacher thought worked or didn't. At this time, I give the teacher a sense of what my expectations for the lesson are, what kinds of things I hope the students will put into their work. If, for example, a part of the lesson has been to ask the students to think about specific ways of describing (simile, metaphor, using the senses in writing) or to think about certain formal ideas (the mixing of short and long lines for effect, or the use of repetition, or to write a poem made out of questions), I let the teacher know this so that he or she can consider those issues when responding to the writing. But I also remind the teacher that I'm not necessarily "looking" for anything in particular, that there is no "what the poet asked you to write" and that the main part of the process is to let the students be inspired to write what the students want to write. I've found that this early writing time is also a good time to talk with teachers about how to follow up the lesson during the week and to see what kind of planning we need to do for our following session.

After talking with the teacher, I walk around the classroom again. If students don't mind, I read over their shoulders, occasionally offering specific comments about what I like in these drafts and why ("The way you described the sky here reminds me of late nights in Colorado, I love that"). If there's something I don't understand in the writing, I ask about it.

After a little more time, I sit down at a spot where the students who've finished can come and see me. The teacher will usually do the same, on the other side of the classroom. For classroom management reasons, I usually request that no more than two students be with me (or the teacher) at any given time (one person working with me, one person waiting). When the students show me the poems, there are a number of things I look for, such as how the student has responded to the lesson. Does a poem about the seasons give me a real sense of the seasons? Does a poem about time really wonder about what time is, how it affects us? In writing about identity, do I get to know who the poet is?

When reading over the poems, I also look for some of the things I know I value in poetry: clarity, imagery, and word selection, as well as craziness/wildness, humor, specificity, use of line (when relevant), truthfulness (when relevant), connections and disconnections between ideas and moments, experimentation with form and language, a sense that the poet is daring to do something he or she may never have done before.*

Mainly, however, when I read the work, I try to look for what I think of as the promise of the draft. What does it seem the writer is promising to do? Does the poem promise to talk about camping and night sounds, but become a poem about reading comic books? Or does it stay within itself and deliver what it initially suggests it would? Does the poem promise to be about love and happiness, about pets, and then become one about a trip to Florida, with no discernible reason for the jump? I'm not suggesting that a poem can't shift in all kinds of directions. I think shifts can be wonderful; the question is, are the shifts part of the promise of the poem?

Finding the promise in the poem might take a few readings. I begin by asking myself if I understood what's going on in the poem. Did I enjoy what I read? Did I learn something? To get a sense of how the student is working, I look at how the poem starts, develops, and ends, and at how the poet made those transitions. I try to get a sense of how the poem works: is it focused and specific, random and abstract? These are questions for myself as a reader and, just as important, as a teacher. I want my students to understand how they write. I want them to be aware of what they are doing, to know their own intentions better. Since I have them with me, I'm able to find out if what I'm thinking about in the poem is what they are thinking about. I ask them: Did you mean to be focused? Did you mean to be random? Did you want this poem to be this silly or this serious? I ask them why they use the words they use. The answers will vary: some students will stare at me blankly ("I don't know"), others are very specific ("Because I like the way that word sounds"). Sometimes their poems will have wonderful accidents in them: one student wrote "the worm crrpt." He meant "the worm crept." I read "the worm chirped." After talking about *crept* and *chirped*, he decided he liked *chirped*

---

* I recommend that every teacher of writing make a list of what he or she values in good writing.

because he thought it gave the worm the ability to make an impossible (for it) kind of sound and he liked the funny strangeness of it.

Once I think I've understood the poem, I make comments to the poet on what seems strong to me. I raise questions about what doesn't. I give the poet a chance to respond. He or she may agree with me or disagree, may say, "Oh, yeah!" or "But I really like it this way." After we've talked these things through (the conversation might last a minute, it might last five), I ask the student to go back and reread the poem, possibly to work on it a little more, not to "correct" it or necessarily to follow my suggestions (I pointedly tell all the poets that they don't have to agree with me, they don't have to change a thing), but to make sure the poem is exactly what the student wants.

When everyone has had a chance to meet with me or the teacher (hopefully they're able to do both, and perhaps they've even shown the poem to other students in the class), I give everyone a chance to read his or her work aloud. After each poet reads, I give the class a chance to ask questions or make specific comments. I want them not simply to say "I liked it" or "I didn't understand it," but to say what in particular they liked, what was not clear, and *why*.

Using this as an opportunity to model a response, I also make comments myself, being as specific and as clear as I can. Sometimes I repeat comments I've already made to the student: "When Joey was working I told him his use of the word *instants* over *moments* interested me because I don't think I've ever used the word *instants* in a poem but I've used the word *moments* a lot—I think it's because I like *o* sounds and he prefers the *i* in the word." I've found that this kind of comment, which reminds the individual writer of an earlier point at which he or she was writing, gives the writer some insight into his or her own process, and it gives the other people in the room perspective on the processes of others.

Sometimes, I talk about how I saw students making changes in their work. Then I ask those students to say something about why they made those changes. When it seems like someone has been working particularly hard on revision, when the page is full of cross-outs and arrows, I ask the writer to hold the paper up for everyone to see.

After everyone has read, if we have time (and too often there isn't) I ask the students to read their poems one more time silently, pen or pencil in hand. Is there anything they'd like to change, to clarify? Yes? Do it now!

Afterward, I usually request that the students return their poems to their individual folders that have been specifically designated for their work with me. Having these poetry folders insures that their work doesn't get lost in the tides of classroom life. These folders stay in the classroom. I insist on that for a lot of reasons, but one of the biggest is my fear that when students take work home it won't come back. I want these poems sticking around because I don't believe any of the poems are really finished and that it's only after the students have *not* worked on them for a little while that they can go back and finish them (I usually save the last day or two of my residency for completing that process).

Phase Two: Transformation

Students often want to think of their first drafts as "finished," but I know as a writer that I need time away from a particular piece of my writing in order to make sure that it really says what I want it to say in the way I want it to say it. I also know that some work may never get to the point that I'll want to publish it or read it to others. This is something I also want the students to learn: that working on something doesn't mean ending it, that while the goal of writing poetry usually is to write a good poem, often the process of writing can be just as important as the product itself.

When I begin talking about the second phase in doing revision (the first is the writing and rewriting the students have done in the class sessions), I describe revision as the art of seeing their work again, almost as though they'd never seen it before. I talk about revision as the art of making something okay or good into something great. It's the art of transforming your writing from being a benchwarmer to being a superstar.

At this point, I remind them that they already have done some revision in the early drafts, the scratching out, the changing of words, phrases, and organization. I show them pages from my notebooks, full of writing down the page, sideways, in my loopy scrawl. I describe my process, how I begin by writing everything by hand, going over and over that piece, and then how I enter it into my computer, printing, revising, logging changes, printing, revising, logging changes, printing, revising, and logging again.

Then I wait. I wait one week, two weeks, three. Sometimes I wait three months, even a year. I talk about writers who have spent years revising manuscripts.

Revision by Addition

I then describe several methods for beginning the new revision after all that waiting. I call the first one Revision by Addition. Students like the math sound. Except, I tell them, we're adding words, not numbers. What kinds of words? Words they think the poem needs.

I write on the board:

I saw the sky
It was nice.

What do you think? I ask.
Someone says, It's great. (A joke.)
No, I say, *really*.
Someone says, It's too short.
So I add:

I saw the sky
It was nice
and good and terrific
and pretty and great
and so good and terrific
and pretty and great
that I have to say it was
EXCELLENT!!!

Now is it better? Groans. Why? Because, they say, it's longer but it still doesn't say anything. I ask what they mean. I point at *nice* and *great* and *terrific*, reading those words emphatically. I point out how I wrote *excellent* in all capital letters to show my feelings. Right, they say, but those words don't describe anything, they don't tell why I'm having these feelings. At this point, I agree with them. So I erase all the words except *I saw the sky* and I ask for help. Give me some words, I say, to describe the sky you think I meant. I call on someone.

Put in blue, I hear, put in the sun.

No, I answer.

What? Surprised.

I hate, I say, days like that. I love storms, thunder, dark clouds, pouring rain.

But that's not nice.

To me it is.

Well, how were we supposed to know that?

And, of course, that proves my point. They weren't supposed to know. They couldn't. And, at that point, we begin to talk about words like *good, bad, nice, great, ugly, pretty, beautiful, fine, terrific, horrible*, that by themselves don't really describe. We talk about how too often people rely on those words to describe things but how, in fact, they don't do anything of the sort. Then, thinking about my love of storms, I ask them to help me do some revision by addition.

What do I need? I ask.

Clouds, someone calls out.

What kinds of clouds?

Dark. Hard.

Good, I say, and when you see them in the sky, what do they make you think might happen?

It's like the city might be destroyed.

Why?

It will be so wet. The winds will be really hard.

And, I ask, do you like the way it looks? No one answers. Well, I say, *I* do.

Why? someone asks.

It just seems beautiful to me, I answer.

And I write it all on the board:

I saw the sky
full of clouds
dark and hard
that threatened to destroy
the city
with its wet and ferocious
beauty

I ask the kids which one they like more, the first poem I wrote (*I saw the sky / It was nice*) or the one we've written. Of course, they like the second poem. Once again, I ask why. The details, the kids will say. Describing words, action words. The words the poem needs.

Revision by Subtraction

The second kind of revision I name for the students is Revision by Subtraction. If Revision by Addition is adding words the poem needs, then, I ask, what do they think Revision by Subtraction is? They know: you take out words the poem doesn't need.

Such as?

Well, they say, we just saw that *pretty* and *good* and *nice* might not work.

Anything else?

They're not sure. I write on the board:

I walked outside and then I saw
the sky and then I saw the
sky was blue and then I saw
the sun yellow in the
sky and then I saw two
birds streaking fast by me and
then I saw they were gone

Someone reads it out loud. The students already have an idea of the problems. But first I ask them to notice what's *right* with what I've written, especially in light of what we've talked about when doing the revision by addition. I ask them to notice that there is a good deal of describing going on here, that they can see what the poet sees, they know a lot about what is happening. So, I ask, what are the problems?

Too many *and*s and *then*s, someone calls out.

I erase them.

I walked outside   I saw
the sky   I saw the
sky was blue   I saw
the sun yellow in the
sky   I saw two
birds streaking fast by me
     I saw they were gone

You use *I* too many times, is the response. Another voice adds, Too many *saw*s.

```
  walked outside
the sky
sky was blue
the sun yellow in the
sky          two
birds streaking fast by me
          they were gone
```

Some students are nodding their heads, beginning to like what they are seeing. Hold on, I say, what if I tried this? I erase some more small words.

```
  walked outside
   sky
sky    blue
  sun yellow in
sky          two
birds streaking fast by me
             gone
```

More nodding. Someone raises a hand, wanting to keep the cutting going: *in / sky* and *by me*. Someone disagrees with the first cut. Someone else disagrees with the second one. I hold up my hands. Either way, I say, is fine. The process may sound like math, I remind them, but, at this point in writing, there aren't wrong answers. Two and two is always four, but with this kind of revision—the subtracting of the words that the writer doesn't feel belong there—it's the opinion of the writer that counts the most.

Revision by Addition. Revision by Subtraction. I note that after each one, we often have to go back to the other. We might, for example, want to add some more words to the subtracted poem. Someone suggests that we should say what kinds of birds. Another wants to add clouds. Someone wants to change the yellow of the sun to gold.

Yes, I'll say. Yes. Yes. Yes.

The final kind of revision, I begin, and often someone shouts out, Revision by Multiplication!

No, I say, but close.

Revision by Division

It's Revision by Division.* Puzzled looks. I wait. Then someone remembers a lesson we did weeks ago. On poetic line.

Revision by Division, does that mean dividing a poem into lines?
I nod my head. Exactly.
Earlier in the year, I wrote these four examples on the chalkboard:

1. I looked and saw the blue sky

2. I looked
   and saw
   the blue sky

3. I looked
   and saw
   the
   blue

   sky

4. I
   looked
   and
   saw
   the
   blue
   sky

I asked someone to read example number one aloud. Someone did. I asked someone to read number two—it sounded like number one. Try again, I said. Again, it sounded like number one. I asked if someone else wanted to try it. Someone did, and when reading, paused at the end of each line, indicating the line break. That's it, I said. Some people began to understand what I was doing. Now read me number three. *I looked* (pause) *and saw* (pause) *the* (pause) *blue* (pause) *sky*. Almost, I said. Try

---

* This final kind of revision is one that I've found works with third grade and up. I've tried it with younger writers but, while addition and subtraction make a lot of sense to them, the idea of changing their work by dividing it seems a little hard. Not that I don't talk with them about how to write a poem in lines, how to move it down the page; but handing them three different ways of making their poems better just seems too much for them.

again. Confusion. Then, understanding: the final pause hadn't been long enough. *I looked* (pause) *and* (pause) *saw* (pause) *the* (pause) *blue* (pause, pause, pause, pause) *sky*.

Yes! I said. Now someone try number four.

I (pause) *looked* (pause) *and* (pause) *saw* (pause) *the* (pause) *blue* (pause) *sky*.

Yes. I looked at the students. Does everyone see what is going on? Nodding heads. I told them that just as the sentence is the unit of prose, the line is the unit of poetry. Just as you pause or stop at the end of a sentence, you pause or stop at the end of a line. Any questions?

No questions.

Then I had one for them. Do these four examples, I asked, motioning at the board, all say the same thing? Raise your hand if you think they do. Hands went up. Okay, raise your hand if they don't. Hands up. How about if you aren't sure? Lots of hands up then.

At this point, I closed the classroom door. I took a deep breath (having warned the teacher ahead of time that this would happen), and at the top of my lungs, as though extremely angry, I screamed: *Don't do that!* Students jumped. One or two screamed. They look at me, stunned, worried. Some looked around to see whom I could possibly have meant. And then, in a tiny voice, a scared one, holding up my hands, I repeated: *Don't do that.* Everyone laughed then. In a friendly, casual voice, I said again: *Don't do that.* And then finally, speaking as though to a three-year old, waving my finger, smiling but stern: *Don't do that.*

Okay, I said. Same three words: *don't* and *do* and *that.* But what happened?

The first one you were mad at us.

The second one, you acted afraid.

The third, you were acting normal.

The last you were talking to us like we were babies.

So, I followed up, was I saying the same thing?

Sort of.

Meaning what?

Your words were the same. But how you said it was different. It changed what you meant. It changed the feeling.

Bingo, I said. And that's what arranging a poem into lines can do.

The students looked at me, still unsure.

The arrangement of the lines, I told them, is the poet's way of controlling how the reader reads the poem, how the reader should breathe, where to stop and start. By controlling breathing, you can indicate tone, atmosphere, emotion. I pointed back to examples one and four, noting that the way they were written made them almost opposites. I read example one aloud, fluidly, calmly, meditatively, the long lines suggesting a kind of thoughtfulness. Then I read example four, almost breathless, excited, jumpy with its broken cadences, the skinny lines creating energy as they ran down the page.

I asked if they saw this. Some nods. But for many, this was hard stuff. Yet I persisted. Asked them to look again. I turned to examples two and three. These were harder, but I directed the students to the physical space created by the openness of example three, almost as though leading the reader to look to the sky, by making the space the lines refer to. I showed them how the short lines in example two asked the reader to look and think and seemingly remember what it was the writer had seen: *I looked* (What happened then?) *and saw* (What did you see?) *the blue sky* (Oh).

Could they see this? They'd started to, but a few weren't sure. I continued to explain. You can combine it. You can make a poem start off calmly (long lines), get wild, (short lines or scattered words), then become calm again (long lines). By this time, most of the students had a sense of what line lengths and breaks could do.

So, I say, when we talked about writing in lines, that means Revision by Division. As you look through your early drafts, I want you to think about the dividing you've already done and the dividing you may yet need to do. I want you to ask yourselves, Have I arranged this poem on the page in a way that tells the reader how I want it read?

Final Drafts

Addition. Subtraction. Division. I tell the students that for the purposes of the anthology that we're going to publish, I'd like them to choose two or three poems that they like a lot, ones they feel they'd like to have others read.* Once they've done this, I ask them to do some revising: I ask them to add, subtract (and add again, if necessary, subtract again, if necessary) and to divide the poem into new lines.

There are some groans. What, someone says, if I like it the way it is?

I nod. Okay, I say, imagine that in front of me I have three flavors of ice cream, flavor A, flavor B and flavor C, and I give everyone in the room a taste of A. Tell me, which is your favorite?

They look at me as though I'm crazy. We can't tell you without trying all three, someone says.

Same with revision, I respond. How do you know you like the first version best if you haven't tried something else? You may be right that what you've written is exactly what you want, but how do you know if you have nothing to compare it to?

I write on the board:

why don't I remember
the deep emptiness
of sleeplessness
at night

I tell them that these are lines from a poem I had been working on for a long time and that I had thought were what I finally wanted. But I wasn't sure. So I played a little:

why don't I remember
the hard emptiness
of no sleep
at night

And then, just to see what could happen, I had changed it to:

---

* Although I ask them to do this with only two or three poems (some students do get ambitious and want to know if they can give me four or five: but of course!), many teachers will follow up on this and have their students do final revisions on all their poems. A number of teachers have also told me that this process of addition, subtraction, and division works well for students in other areas of writing, with division applying to sentences and paragraphs; I know that when I've suggested it as a model to my college students for improving and polishing not only their poetry but their fiction and essays, a number of them have found it quite helpful.

why don't I think of
the deep emptiness
of no sleep
at night

But then I had realized I wasn't crazy about the word *hard*. I liked the way the word *deep* went with *sleep*. And looking over what I now had, I realized too that I missed the rhythm of sleeplessness and emptiness with one on top of the other. And it wasn't thinking I'd been doing, it really was remembering.

why don't I remember
the deep emptiness
of sleeplessness
at night

The lines were back to being exactly as they had been before, but now I knew why I liked them that way.

Revision, I tell the students, is the art of playing with the possibilities of your poem. Now, go, I say, start revising. Have some fun!

Which they do. In becoming more aware of what revision is and what it can do for their writing, they become more comfortable with seeing the lengthy process as a necessary part of their writing, and not as additional work that someone else says they have to do. And with that, they're on their way to becoming better writers.

Appendix 1

The Teachers & Writers Collaborative Fieldcourse

I. The Evolution of the Course

In the fall of 1986, several of my students at Eugene Lang College, who knew of the work I did for Teachers & Writers Collaborative, approached me about the possibility of their doing internships in the schools with other teaching artists. Since internship work and independent study is part of the Lang academic program, the idea seemed like a good one.

With the support of Teachers & Writers Collaborative director Nancy Larson Shapiro, my Lang students began their internships in the spring of 1987, helping T&W writers in New York City schools and gaining some insight into writing and teaching. For the semester, they would receive between two and four credits, depending on the work they did. They would give extra attention to students who needed it, or would work with small groups off to the side. Interns would also type poems, help with assembling anthologies, and the like. Eugene Lang College would designate the internships as a group independent study. That meant the group would meet weekly to talk about their experiences.

The Lang interns seemed to enjoy the work, talking passionately about what was happening. They brought in copies of the students' poems and compared notes on how the writers with whom they worked approached a class. They talked about the teachers and administrators, sometimes positively, sometimes negatively. They spent a lot of time trying to figure out what was happening, why some classes work well and others do not. Sometimes artists would give interns the chance to teach a lesson; we'd all see the nervousness the week before, as the intern talked about what he or she hoped would happen, and the joy (and occasional disappointment) the following week, after the lesson (It worked! It worked! It worked!). Some of the students even developed mentor relationships with their artists, meeting on evenings or weekends to read and talk about the poetry and fiction the Lang students were working on for writing classes or on their own.

The group independent study continued for several more semesters. As it went on, though, students began to express the concern that, although they were having great experiences, they weren't always sure they felt prepared for them. Because everything felt so new and exciting to them, it was as though they weren't always sure exactly what they were excited about. With no frame of reference, other than their own memories of school and the anecdotes of their fellow interns, it was hard for them to get a complete sense of what was going on. They wanted to put their experiences in context. They wanted more background.

I decided to have them do some reading, but not too much, because this was still a two-to-four credit internship for which they already were doing a lot of work. First, we read parts of Kenneth Koch's *Wishes, Lies and Dreams* and *Rose, Where Did You Get That Red?* This gave them a sense of some of the things a writing teacher can do in the classroom. It also helped them see how they could think about the work they were doing in the schools in a broader and more general way. *Wishes* and *Rose* gave them a sense of the early days of the arts-in-education movement, the excitement of poets doing the then unheard-of: teaching children to read great poetry and to become inspired by it to write their own. Phillip Lopate's *Journal of a Living Experiment*, which documents the first ten years of Teachers & Writers Collaborative, was a text the interns also found quite useful.

But this patchwork of reading also pointed up the shortcomings of the group independent study approach. It was becoming clearer and clearer that the Lang students needed a lot more to make their work in the schools as educational as possible. They needed more practical information about teaching and writing. They needed to know more about the history of education in the United States (and elsewhere) and they needed to know more about pedagogical theory. So I began to develop a more formal course of study on the subject. That course would not only allow Lang students to continue to work in the schools with T&W writers, it would ensure that they were prepared for the experience.

Thus, the Teachers & Writers Collaborative Fieldcourse was born. Don Scott, then dean of Lang College, suggested the name and gave his backing for a four-credit-per-semester, two-semester course sequence that would study the pedagogy of creative writing. Nancy Larson Shapiro and

Elizabeth Fox, at the time T&W program director, became strong advocates for the course, urging T&W writers to take advantage of the opportunity to have an interested college intern working with them. Nancy and Elizabeth made it clear that the interns were a part of the T&W community, and that they were welcome at all artist meetings, events, and parties.

Since this was all so new, there was an odd combination of flexibility and stiffness. The course was a great idea, but what exactly was supposed to happen in it? How was everyone supposed to act? We did have the previous internship experiences to help figure it out, though, and we had a good sense of how to help intern and writer establish a relationship. One key seemed for me *not* to be a hands-on supervisor of each internship. Although I usually initiated the contact with the writer to find out if there was interest in having an intern, and I was always happy to talk to both writer and intern at any time, I felt that it was best to let the writer and intern develop their own working relationship.

II. Fall Semester: Reading for Teaching, Reading for Writing

Developing the curriculum and syllabus was trickier. Obviously, I wanted the students to get a lot out of it. I wanted to answer all their wants and needs—about theory, practice, and history, both for teaching and for writing. I knew that an important part of any discussion of teaching, writing, and learning invariably requires a great deal of participant reflection on his or her own experiences, and that it was essential to make sure that the students' own educational experiences (throughout their lives) serve as important "texts" for the class.

It was also clear to me that there is no single way or even single set of ways to think about how to teach creative writing. One of the great misuses of a book like *Rose, Where Did You Get That Red?*, for example, has come from those who have viewed it as kind of creative writing curriculum in which you cover ten poets and your task is completed. I've been in countless schools that have shown me their William Carlos Williams imitations or their Blake imitations, all nicely displayed on a bulletin board. And they're fine, sometimes beautiful poems. The problem is that rather than being seen as the beginning of poetry in student writing, they're seen as the end: *We've done Koch, we've done poetry, let's move on.* There's no sense in any of this that the teachers have done what is at the heart of *Rose*: to locate the poems and poets that inspire you and to figure out for yourself, as Koch does and models so effectively, how to teach it in a way that works best for your particular teaching style and for your particular students.

Therefore, my role as the instructor of the Teachers & Writers Field-course could not be to say, Here's how you teach, here's the Teachers & Writers way, precisely because there is no specific how and there is no specific way. What there is is a confluence of methods, literatures, styles, and ways of being inspired, which sometimes closely resemble one another, but sometimes are dramatically different. The goals are often the same: to help children, teenagers, and adults write, read, and think creatively, and to show them how to do it for themselves.

This became the challenge of the course: how to introduce a variety of ideas and points of view that invite enthusiasm or distaste, in a context of thoughtful, reflective critique. Additionally, I had to remember that the course was to be a writing class, that students would take it not necessarily to become teachers, but to become better readers and writers of their own work.

Over the years the syllabus has changed, depending on the literature available (there are always new and interesting books on teaching, and there was also a period when Myles Horton's autobiography *The Long Haul* was out of print) and on what seemed to work in any given year and what didn't. If students become particularly interested in certain themes that emerge during the semester, I'm happy to slow down, provide additional time for discussion of these themes, as well as additional readings. This has meant that occasionally we don't get to everything on the syllabus, but the syllabus is still there for students to follow up on their own.

The Fieldcourse does have a basic structure. We begin with John Dewey's excellent *Experience and Education*, a small, concise work that describes the author's vision of progressive education, its value to a democratic society, and its relation to traditional education. We might also look at sections of Dewey's *Art and Experience*. As a response to Dewey's vision, we read parts of Diane Ravitch's critique of progressive education in *The Troubled Crusade*. This critique, which is well written, is one that I find finally unconvincing (though some students do not), and it stirs up a useful debate.

Our discussion of progressive education leads us to Paulo Freire's *Pedagogy of the Oppressed*, one of the more influential books on pedagogy. This is not an easy book—the language is philosophical, the thinking often abstract. Yet Freire's writings on the oppressor and oppressed relationships are significant, as are his theories on traditional "banking" education and on manipulative and cooperative dynamics. His idea of a pedagogy grounded in faith, hope, and love, with its echoes of liberation theology, resonates deeply with my students and me. For Freire, if you don't love, if you don't believe in the possibilities of what you do for the present and for the future, how do you presume to teach?

That Freire's work applies to a certain moment in history is important. Freire's work reflects deeply on the international radical movements of the 1950s, 1960s and 1970s. Somewhat like Dewey, his audience is not necessarily the oppressor or the unenlightened, although they can certainly be included. Rather, his message for those who hope to help others is to beware of the means by which that liberation takes place: oppressor tactics, even for a good cause, are never an acceptable option.

It takes several weeks to read Freire. Sometimes, depending on student interest, we also read from *Pedagogy of Hope*, a book in which Freire discusses how his thinking has evolved since the writing of *Pedagogy of the Oppressed*. I've also found Joanne Brady's *Schooling Young Children*, as well as bell hooks's dialogue with herself on Freire from *Teaching to Transgress* to be extremely useful. Both note that Freire's work is flawed; the binary oppressor-oppressed relationship, and the casting of educational oppression as largely class-based can be simplistic and not relevant to all educational situations. Both Brady and hooks offer important arguments for the need to include gender and race in any analysis of education, and Brady is particularly strong in extending, via a feminist critique, Freire's work into children's classrooms. These critiques, I should add, are highly appreciative: as hooks notes, when you're dying of thirst, you don't mind if there's a little dirt in the water.

Several years ago, an editorial in the *New York Times*, reflecting on certain conservative moments in government and society, wondered if the more liberal and radical values that led to the antiwar activism of the 1960s had, in fact, been an aberration in U.S. history. The story told in educator and activist Myles Horton's autobiography *The Long Haul* (written with Herbert and Judith Kohl) refutes any such view. Horton, one of the founders of Highlander, a southern-based center for popular education and grassroots organizing, was a key organizer in the labor movement of the 1920s and 1930s. Many of the demands made by workers during this period became central to Franklin Roosevelt's New Deal programs. The extensive civil rights organizing, for which Highlander was one of several centers in the 1940s and 1950s, suggests that the Supreme Court's Brown vs. Board of Education decision that separate is not equal, as well as Harry Truman's subsequent pronouncements on civil rights, were not so much acts of vision as they were the articulation for change that citizens had been putting into practice for years. The struggle for change and social justice that was central to Horton and to his work at Highlander continues to the present.

Horton's autobiography is particularly good because it is hopeful and anecdotal. Traditional education needs neither hope nor anecdote because it is so entrenched in our educational system. But progressive and radical thinking, by their very nature, do require anecdotes to prove their points and to demonstrate their effectiveness. Horton's successes do not come out of a system that he applies to every situation. Rather, what Horton and the people he worked with understood was that different situations require different solutions. In order to solve a problem, first you have to understand what the problem is. Which sounds obvious, but too often, when it comes to educational practice, it isn't. I'm thinking here of those who believe that simplistic solutions—the imposition of standardized testing, the idea that computers in the classroom will satisfy all learning needs—can overcome the various and varying complex problems of our schools.

After *The Long Haul*, we come to a point in the semester where the Fieldcourse has changed over the years. In the past, my inclination had been to continue dealing with debates in radical, liberal, and conservative thinking. *Education and the American Dream*, edited by Harvey Holtz, brings together a number of disparate, intelligent voices, offering educational debates on class, race, gender, values, morality, technology, teacher development, and so on. Edited by Lois Weiss and Michelle Fein, *Beyond Silenced Voices: Class, Race and Gender in United States Schools* offers significant analysis, and Lisa Delpit's *Other People's Children* has been extremely influential in generating debate on similar issues.

My tendency, most recently, has been to hold back from teaching these texts, and texts like them, at least during the first semester. There are a number of reasons. The most important one is that by the time we've finished Horton, we're often at the midpoint of the semester; it seems necessary to start focusing on creative writing. If the first part of the semester has been about discussing certain theoretical ideas and historical trends in education, I want the second part of the semester to see how those apply (or don't) to writing.

The next book we look at, then, is Kenneth Koch's *Rose, Where Did You Get That Red?* This book amazes my students. Although the premise of the book, that you can teach poets such as Shakespeare, Donne, and Stevens to schoolchildren is less surprising to them than it was when the book was first published, the freshness, originality, joy, and mysteriousness of the children's poetry fascinates them. There is some question here about why the poems are so good: is Koch's success based on his method or his personality? And the answer seems to me to be some of both. Koch is enthusiastic about poetry, and that enthusiasm does inspire his students. But that is also what good teaching is about: being enthusiastic about what you are teaching, and finding the way to make your teaching methods demonstrate how and why the students can also be excited about learning.

My students do wonder why the ten poets of *Rose's* lessons are all white men. In conjunction with the book's subtitle, *Teaching Great Poetry to Children*, they're concerned that this suggests a bias about who it is that writes "great" poetry, or even what the word *great* means in the context of poetry. But *Rose's* extensive anthology after the ten lessons goes a long way toward helping students reconcile their problems with the possible bias.* And, even if it doesn't completely, with echoes of bell hooks on Paulo Freire, they have noted that these criticisms pale beside Koch's accomplishments.

Following *Rose*, we read two books that seem much more specifically centered on how children create and how we respond to that creating. The first is Gianni Rodari's *Grammar of Fantasy*, a fascinating look at the way the imagination works. Rodari's charming book, filled with a variety of exercises and explanation, works as an interesting follow-up to *Rose*. If

---

* It also leads to a great assignment. While we're reading *Rose*, I ask my students to come up with ten poets they'd like to teach, and to think and write about how they'd go about teaching those poets to children.

Koch's work is about demonstrating the possibilities for bringing sophisticated "adult" literature to children, Rodari starts with the imaginative minds of the children, presenting a variety of techniques, based in storytelling and folk and fairy tales, for writing creatively.

The final text of the first semester is Jack Collom's *Moving Windows*. I like this book a lot. In it, Collom names and describes the different qualities he looks for in children's writing. Using numerous examples, he provides a language for talking with children about their work. Such a language also can serve as a starting point for revision because it creates for the children an aesthetic self-consciousness. And this is the kind of awareness of one's own writing that leads to a sense of how to take what one has written and make it better.

Teaching Days, Writing Projects

The development of the class into the Teachers & Writers Fieldcourse has changed the work the Lang students do in the schools. Most do not begin their internships until the start of the second semester, because they don't feel they're ready to. They want, in the first semester, to concentrate on reading, discussions, and their writing projects of the semester, though sometimes opportunities do come up that match a student's interests so specifically that he or she will begin a residency early.

During the first semester, I try to prepare them for actual teaching, in two ways. The first is in the development of a weekly imaginative writing assignment. For it, I announce some kind of teaching problem: *You're working with fourth graders. Their teacher asks you to do something for African American history month. What do you do?* Or: *You're working with eighth graders and you feel that their work is lacking any sense of the material world, there's no physicality to it. What do you do?* I usually give the students two days to respond in the form of a lesson plan describing what they would teach and how, and what kind of work they would anticipate receiving. I also ask them to think about the problems they might have teaching the particular lesson and some alternative strategies they might come up with to deal with those problems. In addition, I ask them to do the lessons themselves. It's not only a chance to do some writing, but also to get some insight into what their future students might experience. On the day that their lessons are due, we spend a fair amount of time talking about what they've developed, and sometimes we even do one of the lessons.

The second way I help prepare the students for teaching is by giving them each an opportunity to do just that, teach. Each student conducts a class using a creative writing lesson designed by himself or herself. We begin doing these about two-thirds of the way through the semester (at this point, I usually stop assigning the weekly imaginative writing assignment; it is too much to ask them to do both). Each student has approximately forty-five minutes to present a lesson and to have the class write. After writing and then reading our work to each other, we give the presenter some time to talk about the lesson, what he or she felt worked, what didn't, and why. After that, we open discussion up to the class for constructive advice. The presenter takes everyone's writing home and responds to it in writing.

Each student in the Fieldcourse also is responsible for a semester-long writing project. In the past, this most often took the shape of a journal in which the students responded to course readings and class discussions. It included the weekly imaginative writing assignments. For those students working in the schools, the journals described what they did and saw, as well as their reactions. Students could also write about what relationship, if any, they saw between what we were talking about in class and what they were doing or had done in other classes. Finally, their journals served as a good place to reflect on their own writing and the relationship that might have to teaching.

But recently, I've given students a chance to choose the form their semester-long writing project takes. This came at the request of one group of students who felt the journal was too restrictive. One student developed a 100-day poetry project, in which she wrote a poem a day during that period, and did a final short essay describing how she saw her writing changing and growing in that period and how she had developed a greater sense of her own language and work habits because of it. Another student did a semester-long letter writing project, writing regularly to people from her past with whom she'd had little recent contact. Each letter described what was going on in her semester, what she was learning, and how it made her want to know even more. There were other projects: works of fiction and art, and, yes, even some carefully written, thoughtful, inspiring journals.

III. The Second Semester

Although I never know exactly what the second semester of the Field-course is going to look like, some things are certain: an internship, an independent writing project, assigned readings, and a group project that will be one of the final assignments of the semester.

But I don't actually know what we're going to study because this is something I leave up to the class as a whole. During the last few weeks of the first semester, I ask them to think about what they would like to study in the following semester. I ask them to think about the issues and ideas that have come up and that they might like to explore further.

The last classes of the semester are spent devising a general plan of what we are going to do. The idea is that once they work out some kind of basic set of themes or issues they'd like to study, I'll propose different texts, guest speakers, and so on that address those issues. Some students also suggest potential readings and projects. We then start the second semester with an incomplete curriculum that we'll continue to form throughout the semester as we become more and more sure of what we want to do.

These late classes of the first semester and the early ones of the second are often very difficult ones. In planning, one of my requirements for the class is that we achieve consensus, that everyone is satisfied with what we finally decide to study. It's important that no one feels that he or she is not represented by the project or projects we decide on.

The difficulty in achieving consensus is magnified by the fact that students are rarely given this kind of broad authority over what they're going to study. They're used to being told what is going to happen next. What they'll read. What they'll write. What they'll think about. In being given this much say, the students often express frustration. At a deadlock, unable to come to agreement on the course of study, they ask me to just tell them what I think would work best.

I don't refuse this request, but I don't exactly answer it either. What I try to do is get them to look at the problem from another perspective, to see if by thinking not only about what the problem is but why they are having the problem, they might not get some insight into what their next steps might be. Sometimes the students complain about how time-consuming this whole process is, but in the end there doesn't seem to be a sense that time was wasted. They've learned how to accomplish something as a group.

Over time, the students have come up with some fine projects. A recent one stands out in my memory: along with deciding to continue to study more theory, as well as to look at works that document what happens in the schools (we read more Freire, also Jonathan Kozol's *Savage Inequalities* and George Wood's *Schools That Work*), they went back to Kenneth Koch's *Rose, Where Did You Get That Red?* and decided to create something similar but a little different. They came up with a series of themes (poems based on other artworks, pretending, confusion, assumptions, etc.). Each week, every person in the class would develop an imaginative writing assignment built around that week's chosen theme. However, only one student—a different one each week—would get to present his or her lesson to the class. The students would do a creative response to the lesson outside of class, and at the following class they would give their creative response to the presenter. The presenter would then take those and, between classes, write a response to each piece. At the end of the semester, we collected all the writing lessons, a statement from each member of the class on his or her beliefs about teaching, and many of the created pieces (at the authors' discretion), and had them copied and bound, one for each person in the class. There were twelve of us (myself included). The result: 144 model lessons, twelve statements about teaching, and some pretty good poems.

IV. The Terms of Success

When I first approached Nancy Larson Shapiro in 1986 about beginning some kind of collaboration between Teachers & Writers Collaborative and Lang College, I saw it mainly as a good internship opportunity for a few interested students. Over the years, as the course developed and became more integrated into both the college's Writing and Education Studies programs, I wondered at the effect it was having on those involved. T&W writers continue to tell me it works; every year I get calls asking for someone "as good as So-and-So from last time." I know the Fieldcourse has made me a better teacher of writing, because talking with my students and thinking about their questions and answers has given me the opportunity to reflect on my own teaching practices.

Although I've never done a formal survey, I think the fieldcourse has made a difference for the students, too. Two former students are currently working with Teachers & Writers Collaborative, and others have told me they plan to apply as soon as they've achieved a little more recognition as writers. I know of several students who are working as classroom teachers, and who rely heavily on the creative writing ideas they developed in our class. Others have continued in other educational programs—in educational theater projects, community organizing, and popular education, and for such organizations as Americorps and Teach for America. Some students are teaching in high schools, others in early childhood programs. One student works with deaf children.

A good opportunity? Yes, and something more. The Fieldcourse has brought about a series of strong collaborations—between T&W and Lang, between writers and interns, between interns and students. It's allowed for a lot of teaching, a lot of writing, and a lot of learning.

Appendix 2

One Hundred Books

Listed here are 100 books that have been important for me. I don't see the list as a canon, a Great Books List, or anything like that. These are just books that have inspired me, as a reader, a writer, a teacher. I had a lot of fun compiling the list, remembering each book, when I'd read it, and where. I thought about the life I'd been living during each book, perhaps in part because of each book. And I remembered the writing that I was doing at the time, which made me realize how much my writing and thinking have changed over the years and how much has also remained the same. I realized I wanted to read the books again, feeling a little sad because of how reading a book again is not the same as reading it for the first time. But I know that reading a book again and again, like writing and teaching writing, like being with people I care about, is also a very good thing to do.

Although I haven't put the books in any particular order, I did have certain criteria for the list. I decided that even though a book may have been meaningful to me ten or fifteen years ago, it couldn't make the list unless it still held some importance for me now, for both my writing and my teaching. Some of the choices were obvious, such as Paulo Freire's *Pedagogy of the Oppressed*, one of the most important books on education of the twentieth century. Less obvious might be F. Scott Fitzgerald's *Tender Is the Night*, yet this is a novel to which I continually return; Fitzgerald's characters, his descriptions of place and time, as well as his attentiveness to the craft of writing, influenced me greatly as a young writer, and still do. And including cookbooks? For clarity in developing a lesson plan, for purpose, sequencing, and improvisation, I think I have learned as much from Elizabeth David and Diana Kennedy as I have from any education studies textbook!

I also didn't want any writer to appear more than once. Without this stipulation, between writers like Freire, Fitzgerald, Virginia Woolf, and Gabriel García Márquez, I could have completed one-fifth of the list. But this made for an interesting problem: which one book to choose? After a lot of thinking, I decided it should be the book by that writer that I would turn to first if I were recommending the writer to someone else as the work that I found most interesting or inspiring (and not necessarily the "best" or "most representative," distinctions I don't think I could make with many of the writers on the list).

Also, I wanted to avoid selected or collected works of any particular writer. In the case of a poet, this often proved difficult—why choose one collection when I could choose them all? But I wanted to force myself to think about that poet's work selectively, I wanted to place myself in the position of having to make a decision about a particular time in a poet's career that interested me, although with some poets this proved impossible: the work of Keats, for example, which I've known only in collected form. To choose only the great odes or the longer poems wouldn't represent my experience.

Finally, I tried to avoid anthologies, unless, as in the case of *Sunflower Splendor* or *Shaking the Pumpkin*, the poems included were impossible to find elsewhere.

I had a good time compiling this list. Make one of your own, and see what it tells you.

1. F. Scott Fitzgerald, *Tender Is the Night*
2. Paulo Freire, *Pedagogy of the Oppressed*
3. Myles Horton, *The Long Haul*
4. Cormac McCarthy, *The Crossing*
5. William Carlos Williams, *Selected Poems* (ed. Charles Tomlinson)
6. Gary Snyder, *The Back Country*
7. Elizabeth Bishop, *The Complete Poems*
8. Frank O'Hara, *Meditations in an Emergency*
9. Rita Dove, *Grace Notes*
10. Audre Lorde, *Aftersong*
11. John Keats, *The Complete Poems*
12. Walt Whitman, *Leaves of Grass* (1855 edition)
13. Wendell Berry, *What Are People For?*
14. Thomas McGrath, *Passages toward the Dark*
15. Wallace Stevens, *Parts of a World*
16. Juan Mascaro (translator), *Bhagavad Gita*
17. Marcel Proust, *Swann's Way*

18. *The New Oxford Annotated Bible*
19. Plato, *The Republic*
20. Rainer Maria Rilke, *Letters to a Young Poet*
21. Michael Parenti, *Inventing Reality*
22. Pablo Neruda, *Veinte poemas del amor (Twenty Poems of Love)*
23. Virginia Woolf, *To the Lighthouse*
24. Willa Cather, *One of Ours*
25. James Baldwin, *Tell Me How Long the Train's Been Gone*
26. Yasanuri Kawabata, *Snow Country*
27. Basho, *The Narrow Road to the Deep North*
28. Jerome Rothenberg (ed.), *Shaking the Pumpkin*
29. Alberto Memmi, *The Colonizer and the Colonized*
30. Lisa Delpit, *Other People's Children*
31. John Dewey, *Education and Experience*
32. Herb Kohl, *I Won't Learn from You*
33. Christa Woolf, *No Place on Earth*
34. Fyodor Dostoevsky, *The Brothers Karamazov*
35. Neal Postman, *The End of Education*
36. Graham Greene, *Our Man in Havana*
37. Sergio Mondragon (ed.), *Republica de Poetas*
38. Ann Petry, *The Street*
39. William Shakespeare, *King Lear*
40. Allen Ginsberg, *Howl and Other Poems*
41. Mary Oliver, *House of Light*
42. Annie Dillard, *Pilgrim at Tinker Creek*
43. Andre Malraux, *Man's Fate*
44. Chinua Achebe, *Things Fall Apart*
45. John A. Williams, *The Man Who Cried I Am*
46. James Schuyler, *The Morning of the Poem*
47. Ernest Hemingway, *The Sun Also Rises*
48. Jonathan Kozol, *Savage Inequalities*
49. Kenneth Koch, *The Burning Mystery of Anna in 1951*
50. John Ashbery, *Flow Chart*
51. David Shapiro, *After a Lost Original*
52. Ron Padgett, *Triangles in the Afternoon*
53. Mayra Jiménez, *Cuando Poeta*
54. Carlos Fuentes, *Diana, la cazadora (Diana, the Huntress)*

55. Gabriel García Márquez, *El Amor en los tiempos del cólera* (*Love in the Time of Cholera*)
56. Eduardo Galeano, *Las Venas abiertas de América Latina* (*Open Veins of Latin America*)
57. Dante Alighieri, *The Inferno*
58. T. S. Eliot, *The Four Quartets*
59. Ezra Pound, *The Cantos*
60. James Joyce, *A Portrait of the Artist as a Young Man*
61. Toni Morrison, *Song of Solomon*
62. Roger Kahn, *The Boys of Summer*
63. Henry Giroux, *Teachers as Intellectuals*
64. Diana Kennedy, *The Art of Mexican Cooking*
65. Elizabeth David, *Italian Cooking*
66. Isabel Allende, *La casa de los espíritus* (*House of the Spirits*)
67. Thomas Merton, *Zen and the Birds of Appetite*
68. Sarah Orne Jewett, *Country of the Whispering Pines*
69. George Eliot, *Daniel Deronda*
70. Thomas Wolfe, *Look Homeward, Angel*
71. Jorge Ibargüengoitia, *Estas ruinas que ves*
72. Alvaro Mutis, *Ilona llega con la lluvia*
73. William James, *The Varieties of Religious Experience*
74. Michael Ondaatje, *Secular Love*
75. Herman Melville, *Pierre, or the Ambiguities*
76. Nathaniel Hawthorne, *The Marble Faun*
77. Wu-chi Liu and Irving Yucheng Lo (eds.), *Sunflower Splendor*
78. Arthur Rimbaud, *The Illuminations*
79. Michael Harrington, *The Other America*
80. George Wood, *Schools That Work*
81. Jane Lazarre, *Some Kind of Innocence*
82. Gabriela Mistral, *Lagar*
83. Ella Leffland, *Rumors of Peace*
84. William Faulkner, *Sanctuary*
85. Lucille Clifton, *Good Woman*
86. Paul Bowles, *The Sheltering Sky*
87. bell hooks, *Teaching to Transgress*
88. Kenzaburo Oe, *Teach Us to Outgrow Our Madness*
89. William Blake, *Songs of Innocence and Experience*
90. Adrienne Rich, *The Dream of a Common Language*

Mark Statman

91. Federico Garcia Lorca, *Poet in New York*
92. William Butler Yeats, *The Tower*
93. Gregory Corso, *The Happy Birthday of Death*
94. Edith Wharton, *The Custom of the Country*
95. Hart Crane, *The Bridge*
96. Paule Marshall, *The Chosen Place, The Timeless People*
97. Marguerite Yourcenar, *Memoirs of Hadrian*
98. Mircea Eliade, *The Myth of the Eternal Return*
99. Mary Morris, *Nothing to Declare*
100. Jack Kerouac, *Lonesome Traveler*

Appendix 3

Model Poems Cited

Homero Aridjis, "Hay silencio en la lluvia / There's silence in the rain" (chapter 4)

Margaret Atwood, "Dreams of the Animals" (chapter 8)

Mario Benedetti, "Verano / Summer" (chapter 7)

Elizabeth Bishop, "Questions of Travel" (chapter 6)

Lucille Clifton, "roots" and "new bones" (chapter 2)

Langston Hughes, "The Negro Speaks of Rivers" (chapter 9)

Mayra Jiménez, "Ayer . . . / Yesterday . . ." (chapter 10)

Keorapetse Kgositsile, "In the Mourning" from "The Present Is a Dangerous Place to Live" (chapter 1)

Juan Liscano, "La realidad es ahí donde el silencio . . . / Reality is there where the silence . . ." (chapter 3)

Thomas McGrath, "When We Say Goodbye" (chapter 5)

Gabriela Mistral, "Ayudadores / The Helpers" (chapter 9)

Pablo Neruda, "El Mar / The Ocean" (chapter 6)

José Emilio Pacheco, "Ciudad Maya comida para la selva / Mayan City: Food for the Forest" (chapter 1)

Adrienne Rich, "Power" (chapter 9)

Gonzalo Rojas, "Al Silencio / To Silence" (chapter 4)

Gary Snyder, "Work to Do toward Town" (chapter 6)

Wallace Stevens, "The Snow Man" (chapter 7)

César Vallejo, "A mi hermano, Miguel / To My Brother Miguel" (chapter 5)

Margaret Walker, "Lineage" (chapter 2)

OTHER T&W BOOKS YOU MIGHT ENJOY

The Teachers & Writers Handbook of Poetic Forms, edited by Ron Padgett. This T&W best-seller includes 74 entries on traditional and modern poetic forms by 19 poet-teachers. "A treasure"—*Kliatt*. "The definitions not only inform, they often provoke and inspire. A small wonder!"—*Poetry Project Newsletter*. "An entertaining reference work"—*Teaching English in the Two-Year College*. "A solid beginning reference source"—*Choice*.

Poetry Everywhere: Teaching Poetry Writing in School and in the Community by Jack Collom and Sheryl Noethe. This big and "tremendously valuable resource work for teachers" (*Kliatt*) at all levels contains 60 writing exercises, extensive commentary, and 450 examples.

Luna, Luna: Creative Writing Ideas from Spanish, Latin American, & Latino Literature, edited by Julio Marzán. In 21 lively and practical essays, poets, fiction writers, and teachers tell how they use the work of Lorca, Neruda, Jiménez, Cisneros, and others to inspire students to write imaginatively. *Luna, Luna* "succeeds brilliantly. I highly recommend this book: it not only teaches but guides teachers on how to involve students in the act of creative writing"—*Kliatt*.

Sing the Sun Up: Creative Writing Ideas from African American Literature, edited by Lorenzo Thomas. Twenty teaching writers present new and exciting ways to motivate students to write imaginatively, inspired by African American poetry, fiction, essays, and drama. Essays in the book discuss work by James Baldwin, Gwendolyn Brooks, Zora Neale Hurston, Jean Toomer, Aimé Césaire, Countee Cullen, Lucille Clifton, Jayne Cortez, Rita Dove, and others.

Classics in the Classroom: Using Great Literature to Teach Writing, edited by Christopher Edgar and Ron Padgett. Practical ways to use great literature to inspire imaginative writing by young people and others. Among the many models discussed are Homer, Sappho, Ovid, Catullus, Rumi, Shakespeare, Bashō, and Charlotte Brontë, and *The Epic of Gilgamesh*, the Bible, and *Beowulf*.

The T&W Guide to Walt Whitman, edited by Ron Padgett. The first and only guide to teaching the work of Walt Whitman from K–college. "A lively, fun, illuminating book"—Ed Folsom, editor of *The Walt Whitman Quarterly*.

The Teachers & Writers Guide to William Carlos Williams, edited by Gary Lenhart. Seventeen practical and innovative essays on using Williams's short poems, fiction, nonfiction, and long poem *Paterson*. Contributors include Allen Ginsberg, Kenneth Koch, and Julia Alvarez.

Educating the Imagination, Vols. 1 & 2, edited by Christopher Edgar and Ron Padgett. A huge selection of the best articles from 17 years of *Teachers & Writers* magazine, with ideas and assignments for writing poetry, fiction, plays, history, folklore, parodies, and much more.

Tolstoy as Teacher: Leo Tolstoy's Writings on Education, edited by Bob Blaisdell and translated by Christopher Edgar. A collection of Tolstoy's articles about the school he founded on his estate at Yasnaya Polyana.

For a free copy of the complete T&W publications catalogue, contact:

Teachers & Writers Collaborative
5 Union Square West, New York, NY 10003-3306
tel. (toll-free) 888-BOOKS-TW
Visit our World Wide Web site at www.twc.org